T0316728

The Little Book of Writing Better

George Grätzer

The Little Book
of Writing Better

Springer

George Grätzer
Toronto, ON, Canada

ISBN 978-3-031-76165-2   ISBN 978-3-031-76166-9   (eBook)
https://doi.org/10.1007/978-3-031-76166-9

This Springer imprint is published by the registered company Springer Nature Switzerland AG
The registered company address is: Gewerbestrasse 11, 6330 Cham, Switzerland

If disposing of this product, please recycle the paper.

The original version of the book has been revised: The Copyright year has been corrected to 2024.
A correction to this book can be found at: https://doi.org/10.1007/978-3-031-76166-9_22

Contents

Introduction

Math into LATEX (Springer, 1993, 1995, 2000, 2007, 2016, 2024) is the title of my comprehensive book on the mathematical typesetting system LATEX. Naturally, I chose the title *The Little Book of Math into English* (MiE, Springer, 2024) for my English grammar book aimed at mathematicians.

This new book is based on MiE but is written for a general audience. While the structure is similar, the material has been reorganized by *Parts*. In MiE, 90% of the content consists of examples and exercises. They have been entirely rewritten for this book.

Stepping away from the intimidating lengths of typical English grammar books, which range from 400 to 1800 pages,[1] this guide presents a concise and friendly approach. My goal isn't to overwhelm you with extensive grammar rules, but to provide key insights that are directly relevant and easily applicable.

I avoid the complex jargon of standard grammar guides. I aim to sim-

Figure 1: Fat grammar books (Vecteezy Library)

plify the process by selecting a handful of essential topics, ranging from propositions to transition words.

---

[1] R. Huddleston and G. K. Pullum, The Cambridge Grammar of the English Language. Cambridge University Press, 2002.

By following our straightforward recommendations, you can reduce up to 80% of the common errors in your publications, thereby enhancing their clarity and readability. Don't worry about achieving 100% perfection—that would require a 600-page manual!

The topics are divided into four Parts.

Part I: Crucial

This part, contaning five topics, lays the foundation of writing by covering the most essential elements of grammar and sentence construction. It deals with prepositions, punctuation, voice (active vs. passive), ambiguity, and issues specific to Russian speakers.

Figure 2: The four Parts (Vecteezy Library)

Part II: Very Important

This part contains six—slightly more advanced— topics that are very important for refining writing and ensuring clarity. It covers conjunctions, transitions, avoiding dangling modifiers, correct use of hyphens, the distinction between direct and indirect speech, and the use of dashes.

Part III: Important

This part contains six topics, addressing common issues that are important for polished writing. It delves into extended uses of transition words, avoiding run-on sentences, the precise placement of only, comma usage before if, distinctions between similar terms, and the correct use of verb forms.

Part IV: And Some More

This final part covers four more additional nuanced topics that are useful for fine-tuning writing. It includes discussions on conjunctions, verb forms, distinctions between terms, subtle punctuation issues, and specific sentence modifiers.

Each topic has a section, *Practice Makes Perfect*, offering exercises and hints. The next section, *PMP Solutions*, gives the answers.

This book is **exercise-centric**. I explain something new and show a few examples. For this to stick, you have to do a lot of exercises! This book contains 640 exercises. Had I not hated subtitles, *An Exercise-Centric Approach* would've been the subtitle I chose.

Figure 3: Illustration library (Vecteezy Library)

I suggest adopting a manageable strategy: focus on one topic per day or every couple of days. Just a few minutes of easy reading can significantly improve your writing skills. Plenty of examples will guide you along—grammatically correct examples are marked with a 'smiling meme' 😊, while incorrect ones are marked with a 'sad meme' 😩. This approach gives you ample time to work through the exercises.

"What is the use of a book without pictures or conversations?" Alice thought in Lewis Carroll's *Through the Looking Glass* (Macmillan Publishers, 1871). To lighten the reading, I incorporated many illustrations and also some conversations (with the generative artificial intelligence system ChatGPT). The illustrations in this book are meant to provide *visual relief* from pages and pages of text.

Apart from a few photos, most illustrations are from the Vecteezy library, which houses millions. Subscribers have unlimited downloads and full commercial rights with no required attribution. Nevertheless, I acknowledge each illustration.

I asked ChatGPT:

I am writing a book to improve the use of written English. Am I crazy?

And the answer:

Not at all! Writing a book to teach better written English is an excellent idea and addresses a vital need.

Encouraging indeed.

For Whom the Bell Tolls

This is the title of Ernest Hemingway's famous novel (Charles Scribner's Sons, 1940). The quote is from John Donne's Meditation XVII.

This book is primarily intended for those whose native language is not English, though native English speakers will also find value in some sections. Where American and British customs diverge, I adhere to American conventions to maintain simplicity.

Figure 4: For Whom the Bell Tolls (movie poster)(Vecteezy Library)

This *Introduction* is followed by the *Overview*, which lists the four Parts and the twenty Topics covered in this book, along with a brief description of each part and topic. I strongly recommend reading the *Overview* to familiarize yourself with the book's content, so you'll know where to turn when you need assistance.

Have fun and enjoy this journey toward clearer, more effective writing.

Barbara Beeton graciously reviewed the draft, and as always, I am deeply indebted to her.

George Grätzer

Overview

Part I Crucial

This part, contaning five topics, lays the foundation of writing by covering the most essential elements of grammar and sentence construction. It deals with prepositions, punctuation, voice (active vs. passive), ambiguity, and issues specific to Russian speakers.

Topic 1: On, In, Next... Prepositions

This topic discusses common prepositions such as 'in,' 'on,' and 'next to,' which are crucial for linking nouns, pronouns, or phrases to other words in a sentence. Emphasis is placed on using prepositions correctly to avoid ambiguity and ensure clear communication.

Topic 2: Punctuation

Punctuation marks are essential tools for structuring sentences and delivering precise meaning. This topic covers the correct use of commas, semicolons, colons, and other punctuation marks, focusing on avoiding common errors and improving clarity.

Topic 3: Active vs. Passive

Learn the differences between active and passive voice and how each impacts tone, style, and clarity. This topic encourages using the active voice for directness, while showing when passive constructions are appropriate.

Topic 4: Ambiguity

Ambiguity in writing can lead to misunderstandings. This topic explains how to identify and remove unclear language, helping you write more precisely so that your intended meaning is always understood.

Topic 5: For Russian Speakers

This topic addresses common grammar challenges specific to Russian speakers learning English, with practical advice on avoiding typical mistakes related to sentence construction, articles, and prepositions.

Part II Very Important

This part contains six—slightly more advanced— topics that are crucial for refining writing and ensuring clarity. It covers conjunctions, transitions, avoiding dangling modifiers, correct use of hyphens, the distinction between direct and indirect speech, and the use of dashes.

Topic 6: So, So That...

Conjunctions like 'so' and 'so that' are important for connecting ideas and indicating relationships between clauses. This topic explains their proper use and provides practical tips to improve the flow of your writing.

Topic 7: Transitions: Short Version

Transition words are key to guiding readers smoothly from one idea to another. This topic introduces common transition words and shows how to use them to enhance the coherence and flow of writing.

Topic 8: Dangling

Dangling modifiers can obscure meaning and create confusion. This topic helps you identify and correct dangling modifiers, ensuring that your sentences are grammatically sound and easy to understand.

Topic 9: Hyphens

The correct use of hyphens is essential in compound words, numbers, and modifiers. This topic explains when and how to use hyphens correctly to prevent ambiguity and improve sentence clarity.

Topic 10: Direct vs. Indirect

This topic compares direct and indirect speech, providing rules for when to use each form. It also covers how to punctuate both types of speech correctly and includes examples for clarity.

Topic 11: Dashes

Learn the difference between en-dashes and em-dashes and their correct usage in writing. This topic explains how to use dashes to set off parenthetical information and add emphasis or clarification to sentences.

Part III Important

This part contains six topics, addressing common issues that are important for polished writing. It delves into extended uses of transition words, avoiding run-on sentences, the precise placement of only, comma usage before if, distinctions between similar terms, and the correct use of verb forms.

Topic 12: Transitions: Longer Version

This extended topic covers more nuanced and sophisticated transition words and techniques. Learn how to use subtle transitions to create smoother, more engaging connections between ideas.

Topic 13: Run-on Sentences

Run-on sentences can make writing difficult to follow. This topic teaches how to identify and fix run-on sentences by breaking them into clear, concise, and properly structured sentences.

Topic 14: Only

The placement of 'only' in a sentence can drastically change its meaning. This topic explains how to position 'only' correctly in different contexts to ensure clarity and avoid confusion.

Topic 15: Pause: Comma Before If

This topic covers the rules for using commas before conditional clauses such as 'if.' It explains how a comma can change the meaning of a sentence and provides strategies to avoid common pitfalls.

Topic 16: Faster and Fastest

Word pairs like 'maybe' vs. 'may be' and 'further' vs. 'farther' are often confused. This topic breaks down these frequently confused terms and provides guidance on how to choose the correct word in context.

Topic 17: To Go or Going

This topic explores the differences between infinitives (to go) and gerunds (going), offering guidance on when to use each form. Understanding these differences is key to writing natural and grammatically correct sentences.

Part IV And Some More

This final part covers four more additional nuanced topics that are useful for fine-tuning writing. It includes discussions on conjunctions, verb forms, distinctions between terms, subtle punctuation issues, and specific sentence modifiers.

Topic 18: As, And, Or... Conjunctions

Conjunctions are vital for linking ideas smoothly. This topic examines the correct use of conjunctions like 'as,' 'and,' and 'or,' helping you connect clauses and ideas effectively in your writing.

Topic 19: Either, Or, Both... More Conjunctions

Building on the previous topic, this section covers more complex conjunctions such as 'either,' 'or,' and 'both.' Learn how to use these conjunctions to add precision and subtlety to your writing.

Topic 20: Less and Fewer, Both and Two

Understanding the distinction between 'less' and 'fewer,' as well as 'both' and 'two,' is important for grammatical accuracy. This topic provides rules and examples to help you use these terms correctly.

Topic 21: Modifications

Modifiers add detail and precision to writing, but they can create confusion if misused. This topic explains how to use modifiers effectively and avoid common mistakes like misplaced or dangling modifiers.

PART I

Crucial

On, In, Next. . . Prepositions

This topic discusses common prepositions, such as 'in', 'on', and 'next to', which are crucial for linking nouns, pronouns, or phrases to other words within a sentence. It emphasizes the importance of using prepositions correctly to avoid ambiguity and ensure clear communication. Readers will learn practical tips for correctly placing prepositions in sentences and gain insights into common mistakes that can obscure meaning. ▪

1.1 Common Prepositions

In indicates being inside or within something.

> *Consider a cat in a box.*

Between expresses a relationship involving two entities with something in the middle.

> *The park is located between two buildings.*

Among is used when the relationship involves more than two entities.

> *She was among the many people at the concert.*

G. Grätzer, *The Little Book of Writing Better*,
https://doi.org/10.1007/978-3-031-76166-9_1

Figure 1.1: Prepositions: in and under (Vecteezy Library)

Across indicates a span or extension over something.

> *The bridge stretches across the river.*

Beyond is used to describe a location on the farther side of a specified boundary.

> *Their house is beyond the hills.*

With respect to describes a relationship of comparison or reference.

> *The painting looks different with respect to the lighting.*

Under is used to indicate a condition or location beneath something.

> *The keys are under the mat.*

1.2   *Using Prepositions Correctly*

Be careful to use them correctly.

> *The package is on the table.* 😞
>
> *The package is on top of the table.*

The correct expression adds clarity by specifying that the package is on top of the table, not merely near it.

She is waiting in the car. 😖

She is waiting inside the car. 🙂

'Inside' is the correct preposition when emphasizing the interior space of the car.

He walked through the door. 😖

He walked out the door. 🙂

'Through' and 'out' indicate different actions regarding how he interacted with the door. The latter is more specific about exiting.

1.3   Placement of Prepositions

Traditional guidelines suggest that a preposition should not end a sentence.[1] However, ending a sentence with a preposition often sounds more natural and avoids awkward constructions. For example:

This is something I can agree with.

1.4   Prepositions with Everyday Terms

On is often used when referring to positions or locations.

Place the book on the table.

With can describe possession or characteristics.

She came up with a creative solution.

By is used to indicate means or methods.

He traveled by train.

1.5   Avoiding Ambiguity

Ambiguity in writing, particularly when caused by the placement of prepositions, can be problematic.

Consider the items added to the cart from the wishlist. 😖

Consider adding all items from the wishlist to the cart. 🙂

The ambiguity arises from whether items are being selected from the wishlist or if the wishlist items are being added to the cart.

---

[1]In March 7, 2024, linguist John McWhorter wrote in the New York Times: 'The idea that you shouldn't end sentences with a preposition has always been an utter hoax. Regardless of one's esteem for any book or person who taught it to you, it's utterly baseless."

The car is parked near the building with the blue door. 😟

The car is parked next to the building, which has a blue door. 🙂

The statement clarifies that the building has a blue door, not another object nearby.

_____

Place the toy inside the box that is on the shelf. 😟

Place the toy inside the box, which is on the shelf. 🙂

It's unclear whether the toy is to be placed inside the box or if on the shelf' modifies where the box should be.

1.6   Practice Makes Perfect

Below are exercises designed to help you practice using prepositions correctly based on the sections covered in this topic.

Common Prepositions in Context

1. The keys are _____ the mat.
   Hint: Consider where the keys are in relation to the mat.

2. The cat is sitting _____ the box.
   Hint: Think about the cat's position relative to the box.

3. The park is located _____ two buildings.
   Hint: Consider the position of the park in relation to the buildings.

4. The bridge stretches _____ the river.
   Hint: Think about the position of the bridge in relation to the river.

5. Their house is _____ the hills.
   Hint: Where is the house in relation to the hills?

6. The painting looks different _____ respect to the lighting.
   Hint: Consider the relationship between the painting and the lighting.

7. She was _____ the many people at the concert.
   Hint: Think about her relation to the crowd.

8. He is standing _____ two friends.
   Hint: Consider the relationship between him and his friends.

Using Prepositions Correctly

1. She is waiting _____ the car.
   Hint: Consider whether she is inside or outside the car.

2. The package is _____ the table.

Hint: *Consider the exact placement of the package in relation to the table.*

3. He walked _____ the door.
   Hint: *Think about the action he performed in relation to the door.*

4. The book is _____ the shelf.
   Hint: *Consider where the book is placed in relation to the shelf.*

5. The cat is hiding _____ the sofa.
   Hint: *Where is the cat in relation to the sofa?*

6. The letter was delivered _____ the wrong address.
   Hint: *Consider the direction the letter took.*

7. The bird flew _____ the window.
   Hint: *Think about the bird's path relative to the window.*

8. The mouse ran _____ the chair.
   Hint: *Consider the path of the mouse relative to the chair.*

Placement of Prepositions

1. This is the tool on _____ you can depend.
   Hint: *Consider whether the preposition is correctly placed at the beginning of the sentence or if it would be more natural at the end.*

2. The story was difficult in _____ to believe.
   Hint: *Evaluate if the preposition placement makes the sentence more complicated or if it would be simpler at the end.*

3. Within the book that we studied _____ lies the answer.
   Hint: *Consider if the sentence could be made clearer by changing the position of the preposition.*

4. On the desktop is the file I was looking _____.
   Hint: *Think about whether moving the preposition would make the sentence flow better.*

5. The decision was something on _____ they all agreed.
   Hint: *Reflect on whether moving the preposition would enhance the sentence's clarity.*

6. Without the proper context, the concept was hard to grasp _____.
   Hint: *Analyze if the sentence could be improved by rearranging the preposition.*

7. With which issue she struggled _____ was eventually resolved.
   Hint: *Consider how the placement of the preposition affects the sentence's focus.*

8. For the company at _____ she works is expanding rapidly.

Hint: Think about whether the preposition would be better placed at the end of the sentence.

Prepositions with Everyday Terms

1. Place the book _____ the table.
   Hint: Consider where the book should be placed in relation to the table.

2. She came up _____ a creative solution.
   Hint: Think about the relationship between the solution and her actions.

3. He traveled _____ train.
   Hint: Consider how the method of travel is expressed in this sentence.

4. She is going to the store _____ bike.
   Hint: Consider how the means of transport is expressed.

5. They worked _____ the project with great care.
   Hint: Think about how the care relates to their work on the project.

6. He answered the question _____ confidence.
   Hint: Consider the relationship between the answer and his confidence.

7. They communicated _____ emails.
   Hint: How is the method of communication expressed?

8. She spoke _____ authority during the meeting.
   Hint: Consider the tone of her speech in relation to the meeting.

Avoiding Ambiguity

1. The cat is sitting on the chair with _____ the cushion.
   Hint: Clarify where the cushion is in relation to the chair.

2. He placed the vase next _____ the lamp on the table.
   Hint: Specify the location of the lamp in relation to the vase.

3. She read the note that was inside the envelope _____ on the desk.
   Hint: Make it clear where the envelope and the note are located.

4. The car is parked near the building with _____ the blue door.
   Hint: Specify whether the blue door belongs to the building or something else.

5. Place the toy inside the box, which is on _____ the shelf.
   Hint: Clarify the location of the toy, the box, and the shelf.

6. The relationship between the variables changes with _____ the parameter.
   Hint: Clarify how the relationship changes when the parameter varies.

7. The book on the table with _____ the red cover is mine.
   Hint: *Is the red cover referring to the book or the table?*

8. The picture in the frame on _____ the wall is from our vacation.
   Hint: *Clarify whether the picture or the frame is on the wall.*

1.7   PMP Solutions

Common Prepositions in Context

1. The keys are **under** the mat.

2. The cat is sitting **in** the box.

3. The park is located **between** two buildings.

4. The bridge stretches **across** the river.

5. Their house is **beyond** the hills.

6. The painting looks different **with respect to** the lighting.

7. She was **among** the many people at the concert.

8. He is standing **between** two friends.

Using Prepositions Correctly

1. She is waiting **inside** the car.

2. The package is **on top of** the table.

3. He walked **through** the door.

4. The book is **on** the shelf.

5. The cat is hiding **under** the sofa.

6. The letter was delivered **to** the wrong address.

7. The bird flew **through** the window.

8. The mouse ran **under** the chair.

Placement of Prepositions

1. This is the tool you can depend **on**.

2. The story was difficult to believe **in**.

3. The answer lies **within** the book that we studied.

4. The file I was looking **for** is on the desktop.

5. The decision was something they all agreed **on**.

6. The concept was hard to grasp **without** the proper context.

7. The issue she struggled **with** was eventually resolved.

8. The company she works **for** is expanding rapidly.

Prepositions with Everyday Terms

1. Place the book **on** the table.

2. She came up **with** a creative solution.

3. He traveled **by** train.

4. She is going to the store **by** bike.

5. They worked **on** the project with great care.

6. He answered the question **with** confidence.

7. They communicated **through** emails.

8. She spoke **with** authority during the meeting.

Avoiding Ambiguity

1. The cat is sitting on the chair **with** the cushion.

2. He placed the vase **next to** the lamp on the table.

3. She read the note that was inside the envelope **on** the desk.

4. The car is parked near the building **with** the blue door.

5. Place the toy inside the box, which is **on** the shelf.

6. The relationship between the variables changes **with** the parameter.

7. The book on the table **with** the red cover is mine.

8. The picture in the frame **on** the wall is from our vacation.

Punctuation

Topic 2: Punctuation

Punctuation marks are essential tools for structuring sentences and delivering precise meaning. This topic introduces the two approaches to punctuation: the elocution method, based on spoken pauses, and the grammar approach, which follows set rules. Detailed discussions on the proper use of commas, semicolons, colons, and other punctuation marks are provided, along with strategies to avoid common errors like comma splices and misused punctuation. §

2.1 Background

The comma's origins can be traced back to ancient Greece, where Aristophanes of Byzantium, a scholar and librarian in Alexandria, introduced a system of dots (distinctions) around the 3rd century BCE to aid readers in understanding the rhythm and pauses in sentences. These dots were placed at different text heights to represent short, medium, and long pauses; see J. E. Sandy, *A History of Classical Scholarship.* (C. J. Clay and Sons, London, 1903.)

© The Author(s), under exclusive license to Springer Nature Switzerland AG 2024   11
G. Grätzer, *The Little Book of Writing Better*,
https://doi.org/10.1007/978-3-031-76166-9_2

Figure 2.1: Aristophanes (Vecteezy Library)

2.2   The Two Approaches

Elocution Method

Aristophanes' method evolved into the 'elocution method' of placing commas, emphasizing the spoken aspect of language, where commas represent pauses, intonation changes, or breaths taken by the speaker. The elocution method is flexible, relying on the speaker's judgment.

The Grammar Approach

In this approach, the use of commas is rule-based, focusing on the written language. It follows specific guidelines for comma placement (separating items in a list, for instance). This approach prioritizes clarity.

Conflicts

Conflicts arise when the strict application of grammatical rules does not align with natural speech patterns.

In the morning, we will analyze the data, and, after lunch, we will discuss the results. 😊

Or simply,

In the morning we will analyze the data, and after lunch we will discuss the results. 😊

In the morning, we will analyze the data and, after lunch, we will discuss the results. 😊

A speaker might naturally pause after 'analyze the data' without the need for a comma before 'and' or might not pause at all after 'lunch'.

The Real Confusion

Native English speakers learn punctuation as children by reading. Non-native English speakers often learn punctuation by reading books and articles.. Neither group analyzes the examples remembered, whether they follow the grammatical method or the elocution method. The result: a mixed approach.

Confusion begets confusion.

2.3 Commas Between Multiple Adjectives

When you have two or more adjectives modifying the same noun, the presence or absence of commas can subtly change the meaning of the sentence. The general rule is that if the adjectives are 'coordinate' (meaning they independently modify the noun), they should be separated by a comma. If they are 'cumulative', meaning they build on one another to modify the noun, no comma is needed.

Coordinate Adjectives

'Coordinate adjectives' are adjectives that can be rearranged without changing the meaning of the sentence, and you can place 'and' between them without altering the sentence's sense. In these cases, use a comma.

Examples:

The loud obnoxious laugh echoed through the room.

The loud, obnoxious laugh echoed through the room.

––––––––

The bright sunny day lifted everyone's spirits.

The bright, sunny day lifted everyone's spirits.

Cumulative Adjectives

Cumulative adjectives do not independently modify the noun. Instead, each adjective modifies the combination of the noun and the following adjective(s), creating a specific meaning. Therefore, you don't use a comma.

Examples:

The dark chocolate cake melted in her mouth.

––––––––

The large wooden table was the centerpiece of the room.

In this example, 'large' modifies 'wooden table', indicating a specific type of table. You can't rearrange these adjectives or insert 'and' without altering the meaning.

2.4   The Role of the Punctuation Marks

Commas

Use to separate items in a list, after introductory phrases, between adjectives, before conjunctions in compound sentences, and to set off non-essential information.

Figure 2.2: Comma-itis—treat it with SA14-14-2 (Vecteezy Library)

Semicolons

Use to connect closely related independent clauses or to separate items in a list where the items themselves contain commas.

Colons

Use to introduce a list, quote, explanation, or elaboration that follows a complete sentence.

Parentheses

Use sparingly to include non-essential but informative details or side notes.

2.5   Using Commas

Commas for Listing   Commas are used to separate items in a list.

For example:

In our grocery list, we included milk bread and eggs.

In our grocery list, we included milk, bread, and eggs.

This is an example of an 'Oxford comma', discussed in the next section.

Commas and Clauses Commas are used to separate independent clauses linked by conjunctions.

She wanted to go to the park but it started to rain.

She wanted to go to the park, but it started to rain.

Commas for Precision Commas can clarify meaning and prevent misinterpretation:

Let's eat Grandma!

Let's eat, Grandma!

Commas with Introductory Elements Use commas after introductory words, phrases, or clauses that precede the main clause.

Before dinner starts please wash your hands.

Before dinner starts, please wash your hands.

Commas for Non-Essential Elements Non-essential elements add information to a sentence but do not change the overall meaning.

The car that was parked outside is mine.

The car, which was parked outside, is mine.

Do Not Overuse Unnecessary commas can interrupt the flow of thought.

The cake, was delicious, and moist.

The cake was delicious and moist.

Misuse of Semicolons Do not overuse semicolons where commas would suffice.

My favorite fruits are apples; oranges; bananas; and grapes.

My favorite fruits are apples, oranges, bananas, and grapes.

———

She opened the book; read a chapter; and then put it down.

She opened the book, read a chapter, and then put it down.

———

He was late for the appointment; because he missed the bus.

He was late for the appointment because he missed the bus.

2.6   *Oxford Comma*

The Oxford comma is the final comma in a list of items that comes before the conjunction (usually 'and' or 'or'). For example, in the list 'apples, oranges, and bananas', the Oxford comma is the one after 'oranges'.

The use of the Oxford comma is a stylistic choice. It can help prevent ambiguity in sentences.

Examples:

I dedicate this book to my parents, J. Frase, and K. Frase.

Without the Oxford comma, this could be misread: the author's parents are J. Frase and K. Frase.

———

Without Oxford comma:

In today's meeting, we'll discuss finance, operations and marketing and sales.
With Oxford comma:

In today's meeting, we'll discuss finance, operations, and marketing and sales.

The Oxford comma makes it clear that marketing and sales are separate topics, not a combined one.

———

Without Oxford comma:

The competition includes running, swimming, cycling and archery.
With Oxford comma:

The competition includes running, swimming, cycling, and archery.

Here, the Oxford comma shows that cycling and archery are distinct challenges.

———

Without Oxford comma:

Please bring notebooks, pens, calculators and rulers to the exam.
With Oxford comma:

Please bring notebooks, pens, calculators, and rulers to the exam.

This clarifies that calculators and rulers are separate items to bring to the exam.

———

Without Oxford comma:

Please complete the exercises on pages 12, 15, 17 and 19.
With Oxford comma:

Please complete the exercises on pages 12, 15, 17, and 19.

The Oxford comma helps differentiate between the page numbers of the exercises assigned as homework.

Style guides vary in their recommendations. the two most respected guides, The Chicago Manual of Style (The Chicago Manual of Style, 17th edition. University of Chicago Press, 2017) and the New Oxford Style Manual (Oxford University Press, 2016), recommend using the Oxford comma.

A True Story

A famous legal case[1] involved the lack of an Oxford comma in a law regarding overtime pay, leading to a dispute over whether certain activities were exempt from overtime.

The sentence in question listed overtime exemptions for 'packing for shipment or distribution' without a comma before 'or distribution', leading to a lawsuit over whether the law meant 'packing for shipment' and 'distribution' as separate exemptions or 'packing for shipment or distribution' as a single activity.

The court ruled in favor of the workers, emphasizing the importance of clarity that the Oxford comma could have provided.

2.7 Practice Makes Perfect

The Two Approaches

1. Which approach to comma usage focuses on spoken language and emphasizes pauses and intonation?
   Hint: Consider the method that is based on how language sounds when spoken.

2. Which approach to comma usage follows strict rules and guidelines?
   Hint: Think about the method that prioritizes clarity and written language.

3. Why might conflicts arise between the elocution method and the grammar approach?
   Hint: Consider the differences in how spoken language and written language handle pauses and intonation.

4. How does the grammar approach handle comma placement in lists?
   Hint: Think about how the grammar approach uses commas to separate items clearly.

5. Which method might a public speaker prefer and why?
   Hint: Consider which method allows for more flexibility in pauses and intonation.

6. In which approach are commas more likely to be used according to strict rules?
   Hint: Think about the approach that follows specific grammatical guidelines.

7. How might a reader's understanding of a sentence change if the elocution method is used instead of the grammar approach?
   Hint: Consider how natural speech patterns can influence the placement of commas.

---

[1] United States Court of Appeals For the First Circuit, No. 16-1901, March 13, 2017.

8. What could be a disadvantage of the elocution method?
   Hint: Think about how the flexibility of the elocution method might lead to inconsistency in written texts.

Commas Between Multiple Adjectives

1. Is the following sentence correct? "The large red balloon floated away."
   Hint: Consider whether 'large' and 'red' are coordinate or cumulative adjectives.

2. Should there be a comma in the sentence "The bright shiny coin caught my eye"?
   Hint: Think about whether 'bright' and 'shiny' are coordinate adjectives.

3. What is the difference between coordinate and cumulative adjectives?
   Hint: Consider how each type of adjective modifies the noun.

4. How can you test if adjectives are coordinate?
   Hint: Try rearranging the adjectives or adding 'and' between them.

5. Is the sentence "The soft warm blanket kept me cozy" correct without a comma?
   Hint: Determine if 'soft' and 'warm' are cumulative adjectives.

6. Should there be a comma in the sentence "The tall ancient tree stood in the forest"?
   Hint: Think about whether 'tall' and 'ancient' are coordinate adjectives.

7. In the sentence "The delicious chocolate cake was a hit", are the adjectives 'delicious' and 'chocolate' coordinate or cumulative?
   Hint: Consider how each adjective relates to the noun.

8. How does the placement of a comma between adjectives change the meaning of a sentence?
   Hint: Consider how commas can clarify or change the relationship between adjectives and the noun.

The Role of Punctuation Marks

1. What punctuation mark should be used to introduce a list?
   Hint: Consider the mark that comes after a complete sentence before listing items.

2. When should a semicolon be used instead of a comma?
   Hint: Think about when you have closely related independent clauses or items in a list with commas.

3. How are parentheses used in sentences?
   Hint: Think about how parentheses provide additional, non-essential information.

4. What is the role of a colon in a sentence?
   Hint: *Consider when a colon is used to introduce something following a complete sentence.*

5. In what situation should you avoid using a semicolon?
   Hint: *Think about cases where a comma would suffice instead of a semicolon.*

6. How can overusing parentheses affect the readability of a sentence?
   Hint: *Consider how too many side notes can disrupt the flow of the main idea.*

7. What is the primary function of commas in compound sentences?
   Hint: *Think about how commas are used to separate independent clauses.*

8. Why is it important to understand the correct use of colons and semicolons?
   Hint: *Consider how these punctuation marks help clarify the structure of complex sentences.*

Using Commas

1. Should a comma be used after the word 'However' in the sentence "However she was late to the party"?
   Hint: *Consider whether 'However' is an introductory word or part of the main clause.*

2. Is the sentence "Let's eat Grandma!" correct, or does it need a comma?
   Hint: *Think about the difference a comma can make in this context.*

3. In the sentence "The professor explained the topic and the students took notes", should there be a comma before 'and'?
   Hint: *Consider if the clauses before and after 'and' are independent.*

4. Should a comma be used in the sentence "Although she was tired she continued to work"?
   Hint: *Think about how introductory elements affect comma placement.*

5. Does the sentence "The book which was on the shelf is mine" need commas around 'which was on the shelf'?
   Hint: *Consider whether the phrase provides essential or non-essential information.*

6. In the sentence 'He ran fast but he couldn't catch the bus,' should a comma be placed before 'but'?
   Hint: *Consider if the clauses before and after 'but' are independent.*

7. Is a comma necessary in the sentence "To get a good grade you must study hard"?
   Hint: *Think about the role of introductory phrases in comma placement.*

8. How does the placement of commas change the meaning or clarity of a sentence?
   Hint: *Consider how commas help clarify relationships between ideas.*

Oxford Comma

1. In the sentence "We need to buy apples, oranges, and bananas", is the use of the Oxford comma correct?
   Hint: Consider whether the Oxford comma is necessary for clarity in this list.

2. Does the sentence "The book is dedicated to my parents, J. Frase and K. Frase" need an Oxford comma?
   Hint: Think about how the lack of a comma might change the meaning.

3. How does the Oxford comma help prevent ambiguity?
   Hint: Consider how the comma clarifies the separation of items in a list.

4. Should the Oxford comma be used in the sentence "For lunch, I had soup, salad and bread"?
   Hint: Think about whether adding the comma would clarify or change the meaning.

5. Why might some writers choose to omit the Oxford comma?
   Hint: Consider how style and simplicity might influence this choice.

6. In what situations is the Oxford comma most important?
   Hint: Consider scenarios where the meaning could be misunderstood without the comma.

7. How can the omission of an Oxford comma lead to legal or contractual misunderstandings?
   Hint: Think about how precise language is necessary in legal contexts.

8. What is an example of a sentence where the Oxford comma is optional but recommended?
   Hint: Consider how the comma might clarify a list in longer or more complex sentences.

2.8   PMP Solutions

The Two Approaches

1. The elocution method focuses on spoken language and emphasizes pauses and intonation.

2. The grammar approach follows strict rules and guidelines for written language.

3. Conflicts arise because the grammar approach may not align with the natural pauses and intonations of spoken language.

4. The grammar approach uses commas to clearly separate items in lists and clauses in sentences.

5. A public speaker might prefer the elocution method because it allows for natural pauses and emphasis.

6. The grammar approach is more likely to use commas according to strict rules.

7. A reader might interpret a sentence differently if the elocution method is used, as it might mirror the spoken delivery rather than strict grammatical rules.

8. The disadvantage of the elocution method is that it can lead to inconsistent punctuation in written texts.

Commas Between Multiple Adjectives

1. The sentence is correct without a comma. 'Large' and 'red' are cumulative adjectives.

2. Yes, a comma should be used: 'The bright, shiny coin caught my eye.'

3. Coordinate adjectives can be rearranged without changing the meaning, while cumulative adjectives build on one another to modify the noun.

4. You can test if adjectives are coordinate by rearranging them or adding 'and' between them.

5. The sentence is correct without a comma because 'soft' and 'warm' are cumulative adjectives.

6. Yes, there should be a comma: 'The tall, ancient tree stood in the forest.'

7. 'Delicious' and 'chocolate' are cumulative adjectives, so no comma is needed.

8. The placement of a comma between adjectives can change the meaning by clarifying whether the adjectives independently or collectively modify the noun.

The Role of Punctuation Marks

1. A colon should be used to introduce a list.

2. A semicolon should be used to connect closely related independent clauses or to separate items in a list where the items themselves contain commas.

3. Parentheses are used to provide additional, non-essential information that is related to but not central to the main sentence.

4. A colon is used to introduce something that follows a complete sentence, such as a list or explanation.

5. Avoid using a semicolon where a comma would suffice, such as in simple lists or between related but dependent clauses.

6. Overusing parentheses can disrupt the flow of the main idea and make the sentence harder to follow.

7. In compound sentences, commas separate independent clauses linked by conjunctions like 'and' or 'but'.

8. Understanding the correct use of colons and semicolons is important because they help clarify the structure and meaning of complex sentences.

Using Commas

1. Yes, a comma should be used: "However, she was late to the party."

2. The sentence needs a comma: "Let's eat, Grandma!" (to avoid suggesting you're eating Grandma).

3. Yes, there should be a comma before 'and': "The professor explained the topic, and the students took notes.' '

4. Yes, a comma should be used: "Although she was tired, she continued to work."

5. Yes, commas are needed: "The book, which was on the shelf, is mine."

6. Yes, there should be a comma: "He ran fast, but he couldn't catch the bus."

7. Yes, a comma should be used: ''To get a good grade, you must study hard."

8. The placement of commas can change the meaning or clarity of a sentence by clarifying relationships between ideas and preventing misinterpretation.

Oxford Comma

1. Yes, the Oxford comma is correct and helps clarify that 'oranges' and 'bananas' are separate items.

2. Yes, the sentence needs an Oxford comma: "The book is dedicated to my parents, J. Frase, and K. Frase" (to clarify that J. Frase and K. Frase are not the author's parents).

3. The Oxford comma helps prevent ambiguity by clearly separating items in a list, making it clear that each item is distinct.

4. Yes, the Oxford comma should be used: "For lunch, I had soup, salad, and bread."

5. Some writers might omit the Oxford comma for simplicity, preferring a less cluttered sentence.

6. The Oxford comma is most important in situations where the meaning could be misunderstood without it, such as in complex or lengthy lists.

7. The omission of an Oxford comma can lead to legal or contractual misunderstandings by creating ambiguity in the list of items or activities.

8. An example of a sentence where the Oxford comma is optional but recommended is 'We discussed philosophy, ethics, and logic' to clearly separate the three topics.

Active vs. Passive

Topic 3: Active vs. Passive

This chapter explores the differences between active and passive voice, explaining how each can affect the tone, style, and clarity of writing. The active voice is generally preferred for its directness, while passive voice can be useful in certain contexts, especially when the focus is on the action rather than the subject. Practical examples and exercises help writers choose the right structure for various contexts. §

3.1   The Problem

Mission Possible: Active vs. Passive Sentences.

Should we choose the active sentence:

Bjarni discovered a new writing technique in 2021.

Or the passive sentence:

A new writing technique was discovered by Bjarni in 2021.

At first glance, the choice seems simple. The active sentence is shorter and more straightforward, while the passive one is longer and more complex.

However, the question of whether to use active or passive voice is a frequent challenge. In academic and professional writing, where precision and clarity are paramount, selecting the correct structure can make a significant difference.

A well-established writer once confessed to me that despite decades of experience, he still finds this challenging. Passive sentences, often encountered in formal writing, can feel natural and sometimes preferable in some contexts.

When I submitted my first book manuscript, the editor initially began changing my passive sentences to active ones. However, upon noticing that my use of passive structures was consistent throughout, she stopped making those changes.

My goal in this topic is to convince you that active sentences, in general, are preferable. But first, let's explore some examples.

3.2   Some Examples

Here is a typical example of a passive sentence:

"It has been suggested that more practice could lead to better results, but this has not been proven conclusively."

Now, let's rewrite it as an active sentence:

"We suggest that more practice could lead to better results, but we have not proven this conclusively."

Jerzy Trzeciak categorizes passive sentences into five types. While he does not advocate for or against their use, his categorization is helpful for understanding and converting passive sentences to active ones.

Let's review these types with examples.

Type 1: "We do something"

Passive: *"This idea was explored by connecting several concepts."*
Active: *"We explored this idea by connecting several concepts."*

Passive: *"This issue was avoided in the previous discussion."*
Active: *"We avoided this issue in the previous discussion."*

Passive: *"A conclusion was reached after considering the evidence."*
Active: *"We reached a conclusion after considering the evidence."*

Passive: *"No assumptions were made about the outcome."*
Active: *"We made no assumptions about the outcome."*

Type 2: "We prove that something is"

Passive: *"The effectiveness of the method was easily demonstrated."*
Active: *"We easily demonstrated the effectiveness of the method."*

Passive: *"It is believed that the strategy will succeed."*
Active: *"We believe that the strategy will succeed."*

Passive: *"It is known that this approach works for similar problems."*
Active: *"We know that this approach works for similar problems."*

Type 3: "We give an object a structure"

Passive: *"The report was organized into sections by following the guidelines."*
Active: *"We organized the report into sections by following the guidelines."*

Passive: *"The letter was marked as urgent to highlight its importance."*
Active: *"We marked the letter as urgent to highlight its importance."*

Type 4: "We act on something"

Passive: *"The problem was addressed by implementing a new strategy."*
Active: *"We addressed the problem by implementing a new strategy."*

Passive: *"The issues were resolved in the following steps."*
Active: *"We resolved the issues in the following steps."*

Type 5: "Which will be (proved, etc.)"

Passive: *"Before the solution was provided, an example was given."*
Active: *"Before we provided the solution, we gave an example."*

Passive: *"This is a summary of the points to be discussed in the meeting."*
Active: *"This is a summary of the points we will discuss in the meeting."*

3.3 Practice Makes Perfect

The Problem

1. Rewrite the following passive sentence as an active sentence.
   "The decision was made by the committee."
   Hint: Start the sentence with 'The committee' and see where it leads you.

2. Convert the following active sentence into a passive sentence.
   "The chef prepared the meal."
   Hint: Begin with 'The meal' and restructure the sentence.

3. Identify whether the following sentence is active or passive. Then, rewrite it in the opposite voice.
   "The book was read by millions of people."
   Hint: Look for who is performing the action and whether they appear before or after the verb.

4. Rewrite the following passive sentence to make it more engaging.
   "A new app was developed by the tech company."
   Hint: Consider beginning with 'The tech company...'.

5. Transform the following active sentence into a passive one.
   "The teacher explained the concept clearly."

Hint: Think about how 'The concept' can be made the subject of the sentence.

6. Identify if this sentence is active or passive, then rewrite it in the opposite voice.
    "The window was broken by the storm."
    Hint: Is the subject (the storm) performing the action, or is it receiving the action?

7. Rewrite this passive sentence to make it more direct.
    "The rules were established by the board."
    Hint: Start with 'The board...'.

8. Change the following active sentence into a passive one.
    "The artist painted a beautiful mural."
    Hint: Begin with 'A beautiful mural...'.

Some Examples

1. Rewrite the following passive sentence as an active sentence.
    "The project was completed by the team ahead of schedule."
    Hint: Start with 'The team...'.

2. Convert the following active sentence into a passive sentence.
    "The engineer solved the problem quickly."
    Hint: Start with 'The problem...'.

3. Identify whether the following sentence is active or passive. Then, rewrite it in the opposite voice.
    "The report was submitted by the manager."
    Hint: Consider who performed the action and how to highlight them.

4. Rewrite the following passive sentence to make it more engaging.
    "The experiment was conducted by the research team."
    Hint: Start with 'The research team...'.

5. Transform the following active sentence into a passive one.
    "The designer created the logo."
    Hint: Begin with 'The logo...'.

6. Identify if this sentence is active or passive, then rewrite it in the opposite voice.
    "The contract was signed by both parties."
    Hint: Determine if the subject should be the focus or the action.

7. Rewrite this passive sentence to make it more direct.
    "The schedule was prepared by the coordinator."
    Hint: Consider starting with 'The coordinator...'.

8. Change the following active sentence into a passive one.

"The students completed the assignments."
Hint: Start with 'The assignments. . . '.

3.4   PMP Solutions

The Problem

1. "The committee made the decision."

2. "The meal was prepared by the chef."

3. "Millions of people read the book."

4. "The tech company developed a new app."

5. "The concept was clearly explained by the teacher."

6. "The storm broke the window."

7. "The board established the rules."

8. "A beautiful mural was painted by the artist."

Some Examples

1. "The team completed the project ahead of schedule."

2. "The problem was solved quickly by the engineer."

3. "The manager submitted the report."

4. "The research team conducted the experiment."

5. "The logo was created by the designer."

6. "Both parties signed the contract."

7. "The coordinator prepared the schedule."

8. "The assignments were completed by the students."

4

Ambiguity

Topic 4: Ambiguity

Ambiguity in language can lead to misunderstandings or misinterpretation of ideas. This chapter identifies common sources of ambiguity, such as unclear prepositions or vague references, and provides techniques for eliminating them. By focusing on clarity and precision, readers can learn to write in a way that ensures their intended meaning is understood by their audience. $

4.1 Ambiguity

Humpty Dumpty's dictum: "When I use a word, it means just what I choose it to mean" (this is what Alice thought in Lewis Carroll's Through the Looking Glass, Macmillan Publishers, 1871).

Ambiguity follows.

© The Author(s), under exclusive license to Springer Nature Switzerland AG 2024   31
G. Grätzer, *The Little Book of Writing Better*,
https://doi.org/10.1007/978-3-031-76166-9_4

Examples

Ambiguous words and phrases, which have more than one interpretation, can lead to misunderstandings.

Examples of ambiguous words:

Normal

The word 'normal' means typical or standard. However, in math, 'normal' is an an overused, yet commonly accepted, adjective : normal distribution in statistics, a normal subgroup in algebra, or a normal line in geometry.

A normal family of complex functions. ☹
is confusing.

Instead of

A normal subring is... ☹

try

A standard subring is... ☺
'Standard' is a good synonym of 'normal'.

Figure 4.1: Ambiguous (Vecteezy Library)

Ring

Everyday: *A ring is a piece of jewelry.* ☺

Math: *However, a ring is also an algebraic structure.* ☺
"He studied the ring" could lead to confusion if the audience does not know whether the subject is a mathematician or a jeweler.

Function

Everyday: *The term 'function' refers to the purpose that something is designed to do.*   ☺

Math: *A 'function' is a relation between a set of inputs and a set of permissible outputs with the property that each input is related to exactly one output.* ☺
"The function of the algorithm" could be ambiguous if it's unclear whether the discussion is about the purpose of the algorithm or a math function within the algorithm.

Series

Everyday: The word 'series' refers to a sequence of events, stories, or television episodes.

Math: A 'series' is the sequence of partial sums of a given sequence.

After completing the series, we left town. 😖
This may refer to watching a set of lectures or solving a series of exercises.

Field

Figure 4.2: Bull standing out in the field (Vecteezy Library)

Everyday: A 'field' might denote an area of open land.

Math: A 'field' is an algebraic structure.

"His work in the field" is ambiguous; clarify whether it refers to agricultural work, fieldwork in a scientific study, or research in a specific area of math.

Integral

Everyday: 'Integral' means essential or necessary for completeness.

Math: 'Integral' is a fundamental concept in calculus and analysis.

Finding the area under a curve requires an integral approach. 😖
It's unclear whether this sentence refers to an essential approach or the math process of integration.

Rational

Everyday: 'Rational' means based on or in accordance with reason or logic.

Math: A number is 'rational' if it can be expressed as the quotient of two integers.

The discussion on rational decisions led to a surprising conclusion. 😖
This could be misinterpreted as a discussion about decisions based on rational numbers.

Complex

Everyday: 'Complex' means consisting of many different and connected parts; not easy to analyze or understand.

Math: A number is 'complex' if it can be written in the form $a + bi$, where a and b are real numbers and i is the square root of -1.

The complex problem was finally solved. 😵
Was the problem intricate or related to complex numbers?

Mean

Everyday: 'Mean' is the average or middle point between extremes.

Math: 'Mean' refers to arithmetic mean (average), geometric mean, or harmonic mean.

The mean temperature for July shows a significant deviation from the norm. 😵
It is unclear whether this refers to an average temperature or 'mean' has another meaning.

Radical

Often, the ambiguity of a word is not binary: general English use and math use. As an example, consider the word 'radical'; it has many meanings across different contexts.

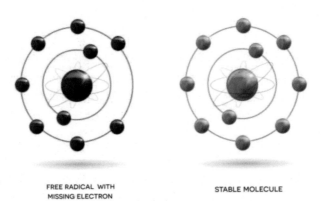

**FREE RADICAL
AND NORMAL MOLECULE**

FREE RADICAL WITH
MISSING ELECTRON

STABLE MOLECULE

Figure 4.3: Radicals (Vecteezy Library)

General Use

In a broad sense, 'radical' refers to anything that represents a significant departure from the norm, tradition, or conventional expectations. It conveys a fundamental or profound change.

Implementing a four-day workweek would be a radical departure in the corporate world. 😊

Math

In math, 'radical' refers to the root of a number, especially the square root.

The radical symbol is used to denote the square root of a number, so $\sqrt{16} = 4$. 😊

Or 'radical' refers to the construct for associative algebras or rings.

Politics and Social Science

In this context, 'radical' describes individuals, groups, ideologies, or movements that advocate for significant, fundamental reforms or revolutionary changes in society.

The suffragette movement in the early 20th century was considered radical for its time because it sought to overturn the conventional norms by fighting for women's right to vote. 😊

Chemistry

In chemistry, a 'radical' is an atom, molecule, or ion with unpaired valence electrons, making it highly reactive.

The hydroxyl radical is involved in many important chemical reactions in the atmosphere, including the decomposition of pollutants. 😊

Language and Linguistics

In the study of languages, especially in relation to the classification of Chinese characters, a 'radical' is a component of a character often used to express some aspect of its meaning or pronunciation.

For instance, the character for 'river' contains the 'water' radical, which suggests a relationship to water.

Homonyms

Words such as 'record' are called 'homonyms': a type of ambiguity where two words sound the same or are spelled the same but have different meanings.

Etymology studies the history and origins of words.

For example, 'record' as a noun comes originally from the Latin 'recordari', which combines 're-' (again) with 'cor' (heart), suggesting 'to remember by heart'.

As a verb, 'record' shares the same roots but diverged in usage to specifically refer to the action of capturing or registering information.

4.2   More Examples

Invalid

'Invalid' (second syllable stressed, in-VAL-id): Not valid or logically sound in the context of math arguments or proofs.

'Invalid' (first syllable stressed, IN-va-lid): A person made weak or disabled by illness or injury.

The proof was considered invalid because of a technical error. 😊

After the accident, he became an invalid and could no longer attend the math conference. 😊

Minute

'Minute' (first syllable stressed, MIN-ute): A unit of time equal to 60 seconds, often used in the timing of math problems or experiments.

Everybody loves the TV program 60 minutes.

'Minute' (second syllable stressed, mi-NYOOT): Extremely small, as in a minute difference or error in a math calculation or measurement.

The experiment required minute measurements of time, accurate to the millisecond. 😊

The difference in results was so minute that it was almost negligible, but it proved to be significant in the complex math model. 😊

Refuse

'Refuse' (first syllable stressed, REF-us): Waste material, not directly related to math but can be involved in statistical studies about waste management.

'Refuse' (second syllable stressed, re-FUSE): To decline to accept or allow, which could be used in the context of disproving a math theory or hypothesis.

The study on household waste produced a large set of refuse data for statistical analysis. 😊

The mathematician refused to accept the hypothesis without further proof, demonstrating a critical approach to the problem. 😊

Project

'Project' (first syllable stressed, PROJ-ect): A planned endeavor, potentially involving math research or study.

'Project' (second syllable stressed, pro-JECT): To cast forward or predict, often involving math models or forecasts.

She led a research project aiming to develop new algorithms for machine learning. 😊

———

Using statistical models, we can project future trends in climate change with a reasonable degree of accuracy. 😊

Attribute

'Attribute' (first syllable stressed, ATTR-i-bute), a noun: Regard as a characteristic or inherent part; for instance, in descriptive statistics or data analysis.

'Attribute' (second syllable stressed, at-TRIB-ute), a verb: Regard as caused by a certain factor, used in statistical analysis or math modeling.

One important attribute of the dataset is its high level of accuracy, which is crucial for our analysis. 😊

———

The researchers were careful not to attribute the changes in temperature solely to increased carbon emissions without considering other factors. 😊

Do Not Misspell

Misspellings are a good source of ambiguity: 'to' vs. 'too' vs. 'two'.

My advice: Do not misspell. LOL.

4.3 Practice Makes Perfect

Ambiguity in Everyday Language

1. What is the general meaning of the word 'normal' in everyday language?
   Hint: *Consider what 'normal' typically means outside of mathematical contexts.*

2. How does the word 'function' differ in its everyday use versus its mathematical use?
   Hint: *Think about what 'function' refers to in a non-mathematical setting compared to a mathematical one.*

3. Why might the word 'ring' cause confusion in a conversation with mixed audiences?
   Hint: *Consider the different meanings of 'ring' in everyday life versus mathematics.*

4. Explain how the word 'series' can lead to ambiguity.
   Hint: *Think about what 'series' refers to in common usage versus its mathematical definition.*

5. In what way is the word 'field' ambiguous?
   Hint: Consider the different contexts in which 'field' is used.

6. What are the two distinct meanings of 'integral' in everyday language and math?
   Hint: Think about the concept of 'integral' in calculus and its general meaning.

7. How might the word 'rational' be misunderstood in a non-mathematical discussion?
   Hint: Consider the difference between rational thinking and rational numbers.

8. What could cause confusion when using the word 'complex' in a discussion?
   Hint: Think about the difference between something being complicated and the mathematical concept of a complex number.

Ambiguity in Specialized Contexts

1. What is the mathematical meaning of 'mean'?
   Hint: Think about how 'mean' is used in statistics.

2. How can the word 'radical' be interpreted differently in chemistry versus math?
   Hint: Consider what a 'radical' represents in each field.

3. Why is it important to clarify the context when using the word 'radical' in a discussion?
   Hint: Think about the different meanings of 'radical' across various disciplines.

4. Explain how the word 'record' can lead to ambiguity in a conversation.
   Hint: Consider the noun and verb forms of 'record'.

5. How does the meaning of 'integral' differ in calculus versus its general use?
   Hint: Consider how 'integral' relates to both essential components and mathematical processes.

6. Why might the word 'complex' cause misunderstanding in a non-mathematical context?
   Hint: Consider the dual meaning of 'complex' in everyday language and mathematics.

7. How can homonyms like 'record' create ambiguity in writing?
   Hint: Think about how words that sound or are spelled the same can have different meanings.

8. In what ways can the word 'function' lead to confusion in discussions involving both everyday and mathematical contexts?
   Hint: Consider the different definitions of 'function' in various fields.

Homonyms and Their Impact

1. What is a homonym, and how can it cause confusion?
   Hint: *Think about words that sound alike or are spelled the same but have different meanings.*

2. How can the word 'minute' lead to ambiguity in a sentence?
   Hint: *Consider the different meanings of 'minute' depending on pronunciation.*

3. Explain how 'refuse' can be misunderstood in a conversation.
   Hint: *Consider how stress on different syllables changes the meaning of 'refuse'.*

4. How does the meaning of 'project' change based on pronunciation?
   Hint: *Think about how 'project' can refer to either a plan or a prediction.*

5. What is the difference between 'attribute' as a noun and as a verb?
   Hint: *Consider how stress changes the meaning of 'attribute'.*

6. Why is it important to consider context when using homonyms in writing?
   Hint: *Think about how the surrounding words and sentences clarify the meaning.*

7. How can the word 'invalid' lead to misunderstandings in both written and spoken language?
   Hint: *Consider how stress on different syllables changes the meaning of 'invalid'.*

8. Give an example of a sentence where a homonym could create ambiguity.
   Hint: *Think about how a word with two meanings could confuse the reader or listener.*

Ambiguity in Mathematics and Language

1. How does ambiguity affect communication in mathematical writing?
   Hint: *Consider how unclear definitions or terms might confuse readers.*

2. Why is it important to define terms clearly in mathematical contexts?
   Hint: *Think about how precise language helps prevent misunderstandings.*

3. Explain how the word 'series' can cause confusion in a mathematical discussion.
   Hint: *Consider the difference between a sequence of events and a mathematical series.*

4. How might the word 'field' be misunderstood in a conversation about math?
   Hint: *Think about the dual meaning of 'field' in everyday language and mathematics.*

5. What steps can be taken to reduce ambiguity in technical writing?
   Hint: *Consider the importance of definitions and context.*

6. How can illustrations or examples help clarify ambiguous terms in mathematics?
   Hint: *Think about how visual aids or examples can make abstract concepts clearer.*

7. In what ways can the word 'mean' be clarified in statistical writing?
   Hint: *Consider specifying which type of mean (arithmetic, geometric, etc.) is being discussed.*

8. How can ambiguity in mathematical terms impact the understanding of a problem or proof?
   Hint: *Think about how unclear language can lead to multiple interpretations.*

Misinterpretation Due to Ambiguity

1. What are the consequences of ambiguity in mathematical proofs?
   Hint: *Consider how unclear terms can lead to incorrect conclusions.*

2. How can ambiguity in definitions affect the outcome of mathematical research?
   Hint: *Think about how precise language is crucial in formulating and proving theorems.*

3. Why is it important to avoid ambiguity in legal documents?
   Hint: *Consider how ambiguous language can lead to disputes or misunderstandings.*

4. How can the misinterpretation of a term like 'integral' impact a scientific discussion?
   Hint: *Think about how different fields use the term 'integral' in varying ways.*

5. What role does context play in interpreting ambiguous terms?
   Hint: *Consider how the surrounding information helps clarify the meaning.*

6. How can misinterpretation of the word 'rational' affect a mathematical argument?
   Hint: *Think about the difference between logical reasoning and rational numbers.*

7. Give an example of a situation where ambiguity in communication led to a misunderstanding.
   Hint: *Consider how a poorly defined term or phrase caused confusion.*

8. What strategies can be employed to minimize ambiguity in both spoken and written language?
   Hint: *Think about the importance of clear definitions, context, and careful word choice.*

4.4 PMP Solutions

Ambiguity in Everyday Language

1. 'Normal' generally means typical or standard in everyday language.

2. 'Function' in everyday use refers to the purpose something is designed to do, while in math it describes a specific relation between inputs and outputs.

3. The word 'ring' could cause confusion because it can refer to a piece of jewelry or an algebraic structure.

4. 'Series' can lead to ambiguity because it may refer to a sequence of events or a mathematical concept involving sums.

5. 'Field' is ambiguous because it can denote an area of land or a specific algebraic structure in mathematics.

6. In everyday language, 'integral' means essential, while in math it refers to a concept in calculus.

7. 'Rational' might be misunderstood because it can refer to logical reasoning or a type of number in mathematics.

8. The word 'complex' can cause confusion because it might refer to something intricate or a specific type of number in math.

Ambiguity in Specialized Contexts

1. In mathematics, 'mean' refers to the average value in a set of numbers.

2. 'Radical' in chemistry refers to a highly reactive molecule, while in math it refers to the root of a number.

3. It is important to clarify the context when using the word 'radical' because it has different meanings in various disciplines.

4. 'Record' can lead to ambiguity because it can mean capturing information (verb) or a documented event (noun).

5. 'Integral' in calculus is a mathematical process, whereas in general use, it means essential.

6. 'Complex' might cause misunderstanding because it can refer to something difficult or a specific type of number in mathematics.

7. Homonyms like 'record' create ambiguity because the same word can have different meanings based on context.

8. 'Function' can lead to confusion in discussions because it can refer to the purpose

of something or a specific mathematical relation.

Homonyms and Their Impact

1. A homonym is a word that sounds alike or is spelled the same as another word but has a different meaning, causing confusion.

2. 'Minute' can lead to ambiguity because it can mean either a small amount of time or something very small.

3. 'Refuse' can be misunderstood because, depending on pronunciation, it can mean waste material or the act of declining something.

4. The meaning of 'project' changes with pronunciation: one refers to a planned endeavor, and the other to predicting future trends.

5. 'Attribute' as a noun refers to a characteristic, while as a verb, it means to regard something as being caused by a particular factor.

6. Considering context is important because it helps determine the intended meaning of homonyms.

7. 'Invalid' can lead to misunderstandings because it might refer to something not valid or to a person who is disabled, depending on pronunciation.

8. An example of a sentence where a homonym could create ambiguity is 'He decided to record the record.'

Ambiguity in Mathematics and Language

1. Ambiguity in mathematical writing can lead to misinterpretation and confusion in understanding concepts or proofs.

2. It is important to define terms clearly in mathematical contexts to avoid misunderstandings and ensure accurate communication.

3. The word 'series' can cause confusion because it can refer to a sequence of events or a mathematical series.

4. The word 'field' might be misunderstood because it can refer to an area of open land or a specific algebraic structure in mathematics.

5. To reduce ambiguity in technical writing, clear definitions, consistent terminology, and appropriate context should be provided.

6. Illustrations or examples can help clarify ambiguous terms in mathematics by providing concrete representations of abstract concepts.

7. In statistical writing, the word 'mean' can be clarified by specifying whether it

refs to the arithmetic mean, geometric mean, or another type of mean.

8. Ambiguity in mathematical terms can impact the understanding of a problem or proof by leading to multiple interpretations, potentially resulting in incorrect conclusions.

Misinterpretation Due to Ambiguity

1. Ambiguity in mathematical proofs can lead to incorrect conclusions or confusion in the logical reasoning process.

2. Ambiguity in definitions can affect the outcome of mathematical research by leading to misinterpretations or errors in the formulation of theories or theorems.

3. It is important to avoid ambiguity in legal documents to prevent disputes, misunderstandings, and potential legal challenges.

4. Misinterpretation of a term like 'integral' in a scientific discussion can impact the clarity and accuracy of the communication, especially if different fields use the term differently.

5. Context plays a crucial role in interpreting ambiguous terms by providing the necessary background information to clarify meaning.

6. Misinterpretation of the word 'rational' in a mathematical argument could lead to confusion between logical reasoning and the concept of rational numbers.

7. An example of a situation where ambiguity in communication led to a misunderstanding might be a contract that was poorly worded, leading to different interpretations by the involved parties.

8. Strategies to minimize ambiguity in both spoken and written language include providing clear definitions, using precise language, and ensuring that the context is well-established.

For Russian Speakers

Topic 5: *For Russian Speakers*

Specifically designed for Russian speakers, this chapter addresses common challenges encountered when learning English. It highlights typical errors in grammar, prepositions, and sentence construction that are specific to Russian learners, providing clear guidance and practical exercises aimed at improving their proficiency in English writing. §

The correct title for this topic might be: for those whose native language does not have definite and indefinite articles ('a', 'an', and 'the'), in particular, Slavic speakers, and specifically Russian speakers. We'll simplify it to: "For Russian Speakers".

If your native language uses definite and indefinite articles, you can skip this topic. If you are a Russian speaker, though, spend a lot of time with the exercises.

5.1 *'A' vs. 'The' vs. Blank*

If you are a native English speaker, you **should skip** this section; it just might make you feel superior. For non-native speakers, especially Russian speakers, the nuances

G. Grätzer, *The Little Book of Writing Better*,
https://doi.org/10.1007/978-3-031-76166-9_5

of article usage in English (specifically 'a', 'the', and no article) can be challenging. We'll discuss this topic in detail.

5.2   Basics

The Indefinite Article: 'A'

The indefinite article 'a' ('an' before a word beginning with a vowel sound) is used in English before singular, countable nouns that are mentioned for the first time or are not specific to the listener or reader.

I saw a movie last night.

Here, 'a movie' refers to one out of many possible movies, and it is being mentioned for the first time.

She wants to buy a house in the countryside.

In this sentence, 'a house' is used because the house is being introduced for the first time.

There is a bird on the tree.

'a bird' is mentioned for the first time, so 'a' is used.

Figure 5.1: 'a' and 'the'
(Vecteezy Library)

The Definite Article: 'The'

The definite article 'the' is used before both singular and plural nouns that are specific and known to the reader, often because they have been mentioned before or are unique within the context.

I enjoyed the movie.

Here, 'the movie' refers to a specific movie that has already been mentioned or is understood from the context.

The house they bought is very old.

'The house' is specific because it refers to a particular house that the listener already knows about.

Please close the door.

'The door' is specific to the context, likely referring to the only door present.

No Article

No article is used with plural or uncountable nouns when speaking about them in a general sense. This rule also applies to abstract concepts and most names of disciplines or sciences.

Movies are a popular form of entertainment.

Here, 'movies' refers to movies in general, not any specific ones.

Water is essential for life.

'Water' here is an uncountable noun used in a general sense.

Love is a powerful emotion.

'Love' is an abstract concept, so no article is used.

5.3   Typical Mistakes

Russian speakers might find the English system of articles challenging due to the absence of definite and indefinite articles in Russian. Here are some common pitfalls and how to avoid them:

Overgeneralization

Solution to problem was found quickly. 😣

   The solution to the problem was found quickly. 🙂
   'The' specifies that we are talking about a specific solution to a specific problem that the listener or reader already knows about.

   Answer to question is simple. 😣

   The answer to the question is simple. 🙂
   Again, 'the' is used because it refers to a specific answer and question.

   Teacher explained concept clearly. 😣

   The teacher explained the concept clearly. 🙂
   'The' is necessary because 'teacher' and 'concept' are specific to the context.

Unnecessary Articles

The happiness is important for well-being. 😣

   Happiness is important for well-being. 🙂
   Avoid articles with uncountable nouns used in a general sense, like 'happiness' here.

   The information was useful. 😣

   Information was useful. 🙂
   'Information' is an uncountable noun, so no article is needed when referring to it in general.

   The nature is beautiful in spring. 😣

   Nature is beautiful in spring. 🙂
   'Nature' does not need an article when it refers to the natural world in general.

Contextual Use

The use of articles can depend heavily on context. Understanding when to use 'a', 'the', or no article at all is key to mastering English.

Introducing new information   *I saw a cat in the garden.* 🙂

   Here, 'a cat' is introduced for the first time, so we use 'a'.

   She found a wallet on the street. 🙂

   'A wallet' is introduced for the first time.

There is a book on the table. 😊

'A book' is introduced for the first time.

Referring to known information   *The cat was chasing a bird.* 😊

Now, 'the cat' is specific because it was just mentioned, but 'a bird' is new information.

The wallet she found was empty. 😊

'The wallet' is specific because it was mentioned earlier.

The book is very interesting. 😊

'The book' refers to a specific book mentioned earlier.

General statements   *Cats are independent animals.* 😊

No article is used here because we are talking about all cats in general.

Dogs are loyal companions. 😊

No article is needed because it refers to all dogs.

Birds can fly. 😊

No article is necessary when talking about birds in general.

5.4   Practice Makes Perfect

The Indefinite Article: 'A'

1. *He found ___ key on the ground.*
   Hint: *Is this the first time the key is mentioned? If so, use ___ .*

2. *She loves ___ cats.*
   Hint: *Think about whether this refers to cats in general or a specific group of cats.*

3. *We watched ___ interesting movie last night.*
   Hint: *Is this movie being introduced for the first time?*

4. *She read ___ book that you recommended.*
   Hint: *Consider whether the book is known to both the speaker and listener.*

5. *He bought ___ new car last week.*
   Hint: *Is this the first mention of the car?*

6. *They visited ___ museum yesterday.*
   Hint: *Think about whether the museum is specific or being introduced for the first time.*

7. *Can you pass ___ salt?*
   Hint: *Is the salt a specific item that both the speaker and listener are aware of?*

8. *There is ___ cat under the table.*
   Hint: *Is this the first time the cat is mentioned?*

The Definite Article: 'The'

1. *___ Water in the glass is cold.*
   Hint: *Is the water being referred to as a specific, known quantity?*

2. The sun sets in ___ west.
   Hint: *Is the west a unique entity in this context?*

3. *___ teacher explained the problem very well.*
   Hint: *Consider if the teacher and problem are known to both the speaker and listener.*

4. *___ movie we saw last night was amazing.*
   Hint: *Is the movie already known from earlier in the conversation?*

5. She took ___ train to work.
   Hint: *Is the train a specific one that both parties are aware of?*

6. *___ information you provided was very useful.*
   Hint: *Is this a specific piece of information already mentioned?*

7. Can you close ___ window, please?
   Hint: *Is the window a specific one in the context?*

8. *___ house they bought is very old.*
   Hint: *Is the house already known in the context?*

No Article

1. *___ Love is a powerful emotion.*
   Hint: *Is 'love' being referred to in a general, abstract sense?*

2. She likes ___ music, especially classical.
   Hint: *Think about whether ___ 'music' is being discussed in general or a specific type of music.*

3. *___ Water in the lake was very cold.*
   Hint: *Consider if the water is a specific quantity or being referred to generally.*

4. *___ information was useful.*
   Hint: *Is the information uncountable and being referred to in general?*

5. *___ Cats are independent animals.*
   Hint: *Is this referring to all cats in general?*

6. I love ___ nature, especially in spring.
   Hint: *Is 'nature' being referred to in a general sense?*

7. ___ movies are a popular form of entertainment.
   Hint: *Consider if ___ 'movies' is being referred to in general.*

8. ___ nature is beautiful in spring.
   Hint: *Is 'nature' being referred to generally, without any specific context?*

5.5   PMP Solutions

The Indefinite Article: 'A'

1. He found ___ key on the ground.

2. She loves cats. (No article, referring to cats in general.)

3. We watched ___ interesting movie last night. (First mention of the movie.)

4. She read ___ book that you recommended. (Specific book already mentioned.)

5. He bought ___ new car last week. (First mention of the car.)

6. They visited ___ museum yesterday. (Specific museum, contextually known.)

7. Can you pass ___ salt? (Referring to the specific salt on the table.)

8. There is ___ cat under the table. (First mention of the cat.)

The Definite Article: 'The'

1. ___ water in the glass is cold. (Referring to specific water in a specific glass.)

2. The sun sets in ___ west. (Specific direction.)

3. ___ teacher explained the problem very well. (Specific teacher and problem.)

4. ___ movie we saw last night was amazing. (Specific movie already mentioned.)

5. She took ___ train to work. (Specific train in context.)

6. ___ information you provided was very useful. (Refers to specific information.)

7. Can you close ___ window, please? (Specific window in context.)

8. ___ house they bought is very old. (Specific house already mentioned.)

No Article

1. Love is a powerful emotion. (No article with abstract concepts.)

2. She likes ___ music, especially classical. (No article, referring to music in general.)

3. ___ water in the lake was very cold. (Referring to specific water in a specific lake.)

4. Information was useful. (Uncountable noun, no article.)

5. Cats are independent animals. (No article, referring to all cats in general.)

6. I love ___ nature, especially in spring. (No article, referring to nature in general.)

7. ___ movies are a popular form of entertainment. (No article, referring to movies in general.)

8. Nature is beautiful in spring. (No article, referring to the natural world in general.)

PART II

Very Important

6

So, So That. . .

Topic 6: So, So That...

Conjunctions like 'so' and 'so that' are vital for connecting ideas and indicating relationships between clauses. This chapter explores the nuances of these conjunctions and offers practical advice on their correct usage. Related terms like 'this', 'these', and 'that' are also discussed, ensuring that writers can use them effectively to maintain clarity and logical flow in their writing.

6.1   So, So that, Such that

So is commonly used as a conjunction or adverb to indicate consequence or result.

> *She studied hard for the exam, and* so *she passed with flying colors.*

Do not overuse it!

So that is a conjunction that denotes purpose or intention. It might be used to clarify the purpose behind actions or decisions.

> *She left early* so that *she could catch the first train.*

© The Author(s), under exclusive license to Springer Nature Switzerland AG 2024
G. Grätzer, *The Little Book of Writing Better*,
https://doi.org/10.1007/978-3-031-76166-9_6

Figure 6.1: So that, such that (Vecteezy Library)

Such that is a phrase that introduces a condition or requirement.

> *She organized the event* such that *everyone had a role to play.*

In this example, 'such that' introduces the condition that everyone had a role in the event.

6.2   *This, These, That, Those, Some*

This and these

> Ambiguous:
>
> *After reading the instructions,* this *becomes clear.*
>
> Clarified:
>
> *After reading the instructions, the process for assembling the furniture becomes clear.*
>
> Vague:
>
> These *are important to remember.*
>
> Specific:
>
> These *guidelines are important to remember when cooking.*

That and those

> Vague:
>
> That *is a great idea.*

THIS

THAT

Figure 6.2: This and that (Vecteezy Library)

Clear:

That *suggestion to start early is a great idea.*

General:

Those *were the best times of my life.*

Detailed:

Those *moments spent traveling were the best times of my life.*

Some

Vague:

Some *people agree with the decision.*

Precise:

Some *people, especially those directly affected, agree with the decision.*

General:

Some *of the best inventions were created by accident.*

Specific:

Some *of the best inventions, such as the microwave oven, were created by accident.*

6.3   *This or That*

The clarity of 'this' versus 'that' isn't always obvious. The reason lies in the context and the author's relationship to the subject matter.

Here's a simplified guide.

Proximity in space or time 'This' is used to refer to something that is physically or temporally (with regard to time) near. For example, in "This cup of coffee on the table is mine."

'This' points to a cup of coffee that is close to the author.

'That' refers to something that is further away in space or time. For example, "That tree in the park is beautiful." where 'that' is used to talk about a tree far from the speaker.

Specificity and emphasis 'This' can be used to highlight a specific item or detail, often drawing attention to its importance or relevance at the moment. For instance, "This opportunity could change your life," emphasizes the importance of the current moment.

'That' can reference something previously mentioned or known, but it is not the immediate focus. For example, "Remember that trip we took last year? That was unforgettable," where 'that' refers back to a specific event mentioned.

Abstract ideas When referring to concepts, ideas, or experiences, both 'this' and 'that' can be used to convey proximity or distance in terms of emotional or psychological connection, not just physical or temporal. "This idea seems promising" might suggest a new or currently discussed concept, whereas "That theory we learned in class was difficult to understand" points to a more distant or past concept.

More examples

To complete this task, you need to follow the instructions carefully. This step is crucial for success.

───────

After following that step, you can move on to the next part.

───────

In this context, 'this' refers to a step or part of the process currently being explained or focused on, making it feel more immediate. 'That' refers to a step that has been previously mentioned or is considered already understood or completed, placing it at a conceptual distance.

To solve this problem, we first need to understand the situation.

That assumption we made earlier? It helps us reach the right conclusion.

'This' is used to focus on the current step or element of the process being developed or assumed. 'That' references an earlier step or assumption, suggesting its importance in reaching the conclusion.

Figure 6.3: The decision-making process (Vecteezy Library)

Let's consider a decision-making process. If a decision is made based on thorough research, then this decision is significant because of that process.

It's unclear what 'this decision' refers to specifically (is it the act of deciding or the decision itself?), and 'that process' is vague (does it refer to the research process or the decision-making process?).

Let's consider a decision-making process. If a decision is made based on thorough research, then the decision itself is significant because of its defining process.

When choosing between options, this can lead to better outcomes. This indicates careful consideration.

The first 'this' vaguely refers to the scenario of choosing between options, but it's not clearly connected to the outcomes. The second 'this' refers to the earlier process but it's not explicitly tied to the logic leading to the conclusion about outcomes.

Choosing between options carefully can lead to better outcomes. Careful consideration of options ensures the best choice.

6.4   Which and That

Restrictive vs. Non-restrictive Clauses

A 'restrictive clause' provides information crucial to the meaning of the sentence. If a restrictive clause is removed, the meaning of the sentence changes significantly. A restrictive clause is not set off by commas and often uses 'that'.

A 'non-restrictive clause' adds extra information to the sentence, which is not critical to understanding it. Removing a non-restrictive clause does not change the meaning of the sentence. These clauses are usually set off by commas and often use 'which'.

Using 'That'

Restrictive clause:

> *The book* that *changed my life is on the shelf.*

Here, "that changed my life" is a restrictive clause because it specifies the particular book being discussed.

Using 'Which'

Non-restrictive clause:

> *The Eiffel Tower,* which *is in Paris, is an iconic landmark.*

'which is in Paris' is a non-restrictive clause. It adds information about the Eiffel Tower but is not necessary to understand the main point.

Comma as a Cue

If you're adding information that doesn't change the meaning of a sentence, use 'which' and set off the clause with commas. If the information is essential and removing it would alter the meaning of the sentence, use 'that' without commas.

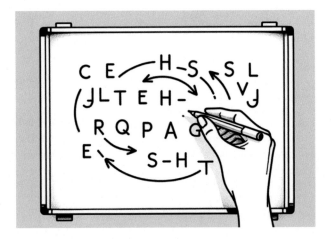

Figure 6.4: Rearrange the sentence (Vecteezy Library)

Rearrange the Sentence

If the sentence becomes difficult to read with the 'that' clause (restrictive clause), try to restructure it.

> Before rearranging it:

> *The article argues that, for every decision, there is a consequence.*

After rearranging it:

For every decision, the article argues, there is a consequence.

According to the article, for every decision, there is a consequence.

If the inserted remark is an aside or provides clarification, consider using parentheses.

The analysis shows that (given the available data) the results are conclusive.

When a sentence becomes too complex, consider breaking the sentence into two or more sentences.

Before simplification:

The study suggests that, despite initial skepticism, the evidence supports the hypothesis.

6.5   Practice Makes Perfect

So, So that, Such that

1. Use 'so' to combine these sentences: "She was late. She missed the beginning of the movie."
   Hint: Think about how to connect the cause (being late) with the effect (missing the beginning).

2. Use 'so that' to explain the purpose: "He set his alarm early. He wanted to catch the sunrise."
   Hint: Consider how 'so that' can link the action (setting the alarm) to the purpose (catching the sunrise).

3. Apply 'such that' to describe a condition: "She arranged the chairs. Everyone could see the stage."
   Hint: Use 'such that' to express the condition that everyone could see the stage.

4. Create a sentence using 'so': "The weather was bad. The event was canceled."
   Hint: Combine the sentences to show the result of the bad weather.

5. Combine the sentences with 'so that': "They left early. They could avoid traffic."
   Hint: Use 'so that' to explain why they left early.

6. Use 'such that' in a sentence: "She explained the task. Everyone understood what to do."
   Hint: Apply 'such that' to indicate the result of her explanation.

7. Use 'so' to describe an outcome: "He was tired. He went to bed early."
   Hint: Link the cause of being tired to the effect of going to bed early.

8. Create a sentence using 'so that: "She saved money. She could travel."
   Hint: Show how saving money was done with the intention of traveling.

This, These, That, Those, Some

1. Clarify the meaning of 'this' in the sentence: "This is important."
   Hint: Replace 'this' with a specific reference to what is important.

2. Specify what 'these refers to: "These are the best."
   Hint: Add more detail to make 'these' specific.

3. Use 'that' clearly: "That was unexpected."
   Hint: Provide context to make 'that' clear.

4. Detail what 'those' refers to: "Those were the days."
   Hint: Explain what is meant by 'those days.'

5. Make 'some' more precise: "Some people agree."
   Hint: Add specificity to who 'some people' are.

6. Clarify the use of 'this': "This needs to be done."
   Hint: Specify what 'this' refers to.

7. Specify what 'those' refers to: "Those are interesting."
   Hint: Provide more details about what 'those' are.

8. Use 'some' in a detailed context: "Some items were missing."
   Hint: Clarify which items were missing.

This or That

1. Differentiate between 'this' and 'that': "This book is mine. That one is yours."
   Hint: Ensure 'this' and 'that' correctly refer to specific books.

2. Use 'this' in a sentence: "This is the key to success."
   Hint: Make sure 'this' refers to a clear concept or item.

3. Write a sentence using 'that' for emphasis: "That was the best part of the trip."
   Hint: Use 'that' to emphasize the specific part of the trip.

4. Compare 'this' and 'that' in context: "This is what we need now. That can wait."
   Hint: Clearly distinguish what 'this' and 'that' refer to.

5. Explain a concept using 'this': "This idea could revolutionize the industry."
   Hint: Ensure "this idea" is clearly defined in the context.

6. Highlight an example with 'that': "Remember that time we got lost?"
   Hint: Use 'that' to refer to a specific past event.

7. Use 'this' to point out something recent: "This decision was just made."
   Hint: Specify the decision being referred to.

8. Use 'that' to refer back to something earlier: "That proposal was rejected."
   Hint: Clearly identify the proposal being referred to.

6.6   PMP Solutions

So, So That, Such That

1. She was late, **so** she missed the beginning of the movie.

2. He set his alarm early **so that** he could catch the sunrise.

3. She arranged the chairs **such that** everyone could see the stage.

4. The weather was bad, **so** the event was canceled.

5. They left early **so that** they could avoid traffic.

6. She explained the task **such that** everyone understood what to do.

7. He was tired, **so** he went to bed early.

8. She saved money **so that** she could travel.

This, These, That, Those, Some

1. **This instruction** is important.

2. **These books** are the best.

3. **That result** was unexpected.

4. **Those summer days** were the best times of my life.

5. **Some experts** agree with the decision.

6. **This task** needs to be done.

7. **Those ideas** are interesting.

8. **Some of the documents** were missing.

This or That

1. **This book** is mine. **That one** is yours.

2. **This strategy** is the key to success.

3. **That moment** was the best part of the trip.

4. **This task** is what we need now. **That other task** can wait.

5. **This idea** could revolutionize the industry.

6. Remember **that time** we got lost?

7. **This decision** was just made.

8. **That proposal** was rejected.

Transitions: Short Version

Topic 7: Transitions: Short Version

Transitions are key to guiding readers through text by linking sentences and paragraphs seamlessly. This chapter introduces common transition words and phrases, such as 'however', 'therefore', and 'in addition', and explains how to use them to enhance the flow and coherence of writing. §

7.1 Transition Words

Transition words connect ideas and add structure to your writing. Here is an example using the common transition word: 'so'.

The weather was terrible.
So *we decided to stay indoors.*

Transition words come in six categories.

Cause and effect

Show the relationship between an action or event and its outcome.

G. Grätzer, *The Little Book of Writing Better*,
https://doi.org/10.1007/978-3-031-76166-9_7

Consequently, *missing the bus made her late for the meeting.*

Comparison

Highlight similarities between two or more ideas or objects.

Similarly, *learning to cook is like learning to paint; both require practice and patience.*

Contrast

These words point out differences between two or more ideas or objects.

On the other hand, *while he enjoys reading, she prefers watching movies.*

On the one hand, *she loves the excitement of city life;* on the other hand, *she misses the tranquility of the countryside.*

Figure 7.1:   Transitions
(Vecteezy Library)

Sequence/order

Indicate a chronological or logical sequence of events or ideas.

First, *gather all necessary ingredients.* Next, *follow the recipe carefully.* Finally, *serve the dish while it's hot.*

Example/emphasis

Introduce examples or highlight important points or ideas.

For instance, *regular exercise can significantly improve mental health.*

Figure 7.2: Dice (Vecteezy Library)

Conclusion/summary

Signal the end of a discussion and often introduce a summary or conclusion.

In summary, *a balanced diet and regular exercise are key to maintaining good health.*

We'll discuss these in Topic 12.

Choose your transitions carefully to ensure they accurately reflect the relationship between the ideas you are connecting.

Vary your transition words and phrases. Overusing a single transition, such as 'so', can make your writing feel repetitive.

Avoid placing commas after short transition words. For example, 'So,' looks awkward. The general rule is to omit commas if the transition word is fewer than four characters.

7.2 Practice Makes Perfect

1. Rewrite the following sentences using a transition word to show cause and effect: "The streets were flooded. We couldn't go out."
   Hint: Think about a transition word that connects the flooded streets with the result of staying indoors.

2. Use a transition word to contrast these ideas: "She loves sweets. She avoids sugar."
   Hint: Consider a transition that highlights the contrast between her love for sweets and her decision to avoid sugar.

3. Introduce a sequence with transition words: "I woke up late. I missed the bus. I was late to work."
   Hint: Think about how you can structure these actions in a logical order with transitions.

4. Emphasize the importance of this statement with a transition word: "Getting enough sleep is crucial for health."
   Hint: Look for a transition word that highlights the significance of sleep.

5. Provide an example using a transition word: "Eating healthy foods is important."
   Hint: What specific example could you introduce that shows the importance of eating healthy foods?

6. Summarize the following discussion with a transition word: "We've examined the benefits and drawbacks of remote work."
   Hint: Think about how you can wrap up the discussion in a concise way using a transition.

7. Compare these two ideas with a transition word: "Reading fiction is enjoyable. Watching movies is relaxing."
   Hint: Which transition word would best show that both activities are similar in purpose?

8. Contrast the following situations with a transition word: "He loves traveling. He dislikes packing."
   Hint: Find a transition word that highlights the difference between his love for traveling and his dislike for packing.

7.3   PMP Solutions

1. The streets were flooded. *Therefore*, we couldn't go out.

2. She loves sweets. *However*, she avoids sugar.

3. *First*, I woke up late. *Then*, I missed the bus. *Finally*, I was late to work.

4. *Indeed*, getting enough sleep is crucial for health.

5. *For example*, eating fruits and vegetables is important for maintaining a healthy diet.

6. *In conclusion*, we've examined the benefits and drawbacks of remote work.

7. Reading fiction is enjoyable. *Likewise*, watching movies is relaxing.

8. He loves traveling. *On the other hand*, he dislikes packing.

8

Dangling

Dangling modifiers can obscure meaning and create confusion in sentences. This chapter explains what dangling modifiers are and provides strategies for avoiding them, focusing on improving sentence structure and clarity. Readers will learn to identify and correct these errors, ensuring that their writing is both grammatically sound and easy to understand. §

To 'dangle' means to hang or swing loosely, particularly when one end moves freely. In grammar, when we talk about 'dangling' modifiers, it describes a word or phrase that is improperly linked to the words it's supposed to modify. In grammar, 'dangling' modifiers refer to a word or phrase that is improperly linked to the words it is supposed to modify.

Figure 8.1: Dangle
(Vecteezy Library)

In the previous topic, we discussed the '-ing form' of a verb. Similarly, there is an '-ed form': we add '-ed' to the base form of a verb. So 'support' becomes 'supported', and 'form' becomes 'formed'. Irregular verbs are exceptions; for example, 'break' becomes 'broken' and 'write' becomes 'written'. A 'participle' is the '-ing form' or the '-ed form' of a verb. This term now allows us to introduce 'dangling

G. Grätzer, *The Little Book of Writing Better*,
https://doi.org/10.1007/978-3-031-76166-9_8

participles', the subject of this topic. We make the introduction with an example:

Determined to win the race, the finish line seemed miles away. 😩

Here, "Determined to win the race" is intended to modify the runner attempting the task. Instead, it modifies "the finish line", suggesting that the finish line itself is determined to win the race.

8.1 Dangling Participle

A 'dangling participle' is a serious grammatical error that occurs when a participial phrase (an adjective phrase that starts with a participle) is not clearly or logically related to the noun it is intended to modify. This usually occurs when the noun being modified is missing from the sentence, leaving the participle 'dangling' with nothing to modify.

Here is another example:

Running to catch the bus, my book fell out of my bag. 😩

In this sentence, "Running to catch the bus" is a participial phrase meant to describe the action of the subject. However, the subject immediately following this phrase is "my book", which cannot run. The intended meaning is that the speaker or another person was likely running to catch the bus when the book fell out of their bag. Correct it:

Running to catch the bus, I dropped my book. 😊

Dangling participles disrupt the clarity of writing and can lead to misinterpretation or unintentional humor. They're often easily fixed by restructuring the sentence so that the participle clearly modifies the intended noun or by introducing the intended subject immediately after the participial phrase.

Using a new recipe, the cake turned out delicious. 😩
This sentence leaves it unclear who is using the new recipe.
Using a new recipe, I made a delicious cake. 😊

8.2 Strategies for Avoidance and Correction

Identify the action Begin by identifying the action your participle describes. Ensure this action is clearly and logically connected to a doer mentioned in the sentence.

Rephrase for clarity Often, the simplest solution to correct a dangling participle is to rephrase the sentence to include the actor explicitly. For example, "After finishing the project, the results were impressive." could be revised to "After we finished the project, the results were impressive."

Restructure with active voice Many dangling participles result from attempts to use a passive construction where an active voice would be more direct and clear. Consider using an active voice to directly connect the action with its doer.

8.3   Practice Makes Perfect

In this section, you will practice distinguishing between the 'to-form' and the 'ing-form', using full and incomplete infinitives, and correcting split infinitives. Each exercise will guide you through the correct application of these forms.

The To-form and the Ing-form

1. *He enjoys to read books.*
   Hint: *Consider whether the 'to-form' or the 'ing-form' is more appropriate after 'enjoys'.*

2. *To swim is fun during the summer.*
   Hint: *Determine if the 'to-form' is correctly used or if the 'ing-form' would be better.*

3. *I prefer eating at home rather than to go out.*
   Hint: *Ensure consistency in the forms used in parallel constructions.*

4. *She decided going to the store after work.*
   Hint: *Check if the 'ing-form' is correctly used with 'decided'.*

5. *To exercise daily is good for your health.*
   Hint: *Verify if the 'to-form' is correctly used at the beginning of the sentence.*

6. *They stopped to talk on the phone while walking.*
   Hint: *Determine if the 'to-form' or the 'ing-form' is better in this context.*

7. *My hobby is to collect stamps.*
   Hint: *Consider if the 'ing-form' is more appropriate after 'is'.*

8. *Going to the beach is my favorite summer activity.*
   Hint: *Check if the 'ing-form' is correctly used at the beginning of the sentence.*

Full and Incomplete Infinitives

1. *She wants to quickly finish her homework.*
   Hint: *Consider the position of the adverb 'quickly' in relation to the 'infinitive'.*

2. *We can to start the meeting now.*
   Hint: *Verify if the 'infinitive' is correctly used after 'can'.*

3. *They might to join us for dinner.*
   Hint: *Check the 'infinitive' form after the helping verb 'might'.*

4. *To bake a cake requires patience.*
   Hint: *Confirm if the 'to-form' is correctly used as the subject of the sentence.*

5. *He made me to apologize for the mistake.*
   Hint: *Ensure that the correct 'infinitive' form is used after 'made'.*

6. *We should to leave early tomorrow.*
   Hint: *Verify the use of the 'infinitive' after the modal verb 'should'.*

7. *I can to help you with your homework.*
   Hint: *Check if the 'infinitive' is correctly used after 'can'.*

8. *She needs to finish her project by tomorrow.*
   Hint: *Ensure that the 'to-form' is correctly used after 'needs'.*

Split Infinitives

1. *To thoroughly understand the topic, you need to study.*
   Hint: *Consider if 'thoroughly' is correctly placed within the 'infinitive'.*

2. *To always be on time is important for success.*
   Hint: *Determine if 'always' is properly placed in the sentence.*

3. *He tried to quietly leave the room.*
   Hint: *Check the position of 'quietly' in the 'infinitive'.*

4. *To correctly solve the puzzle, focus on the clues.*
   Hint: *Ensure that 'correctly' is correctly positioned in the sentence.*

5. *To effectively manage your time, create a schedule.*
   Hint: *Consider the position of 'effectively' in the 'infinitive'.*

6. *To quickly answer the question, he raised his hand.*
   Hint: *Check if 'quickly' is correctly placed in the sentence.*

7. *To clearly express your ideas, use simple language.*
   Hint: *Verify the placement of 'clearly' in the 'infinitive'.*

8. *To fully understand the concept, you must practice.*
   Hint: *Consider the placement of 'fully' within the 'infinitive'.*

8.4   PMP Solutions

The To-form and the Ing-form

1. **Original:** *He enjoys to read books.*
   Corrected: *He enjoys reading books.*

2. **Original:** *To swim is fun during the summer.*
   Corrected: *Swimming is fun during the summer.*

3. **Original:** *I prefer eating at home rather than to go out.*

Corrected: *I prefer eating at home rather than going out.*

4. **Original:** *She decided going to the store after work.*
   Corrected: *She decided to go to the store after work.*

5. **Original:** *To exercise daily is good for your health.*
   Corrected: *Exercising daily is good for your health.*

6. **Original:** *They stopped to talk on the phone while walking.*
   Corrected: *They stopped talking on the phone while walking.*

7. **Original:** *My hobby is to collect stamps.*
   Corrected: *My hobby is collecting stamps.*

8. **Original:** *Going to the beach is my favorite summer activity.*
   Corrected: *Going to the beach is my favorite summer activity.* **(No correction needed)**

Full and Incomplete Infinitives

1. **Original:** *She wants to quickly finish her homework.*
   Corrected: *She wants to finish her homework quickly.*

2. **Original:** *We can to start the meeting now.*
   Corrected: *We can start the meeting now.*

3. **Original:** *They might to join us for dinner.*
   Corrected: *They might join us for dinner.*

4. **Original:** *To bake a cake requires patience.*
   Corrected: *Baking a cake requires patience.*

5. **Original:** *He made me to apologize for the mistake.*
   Corrected: *He made me apologize for the mistake.*

6. **Original:** *We should to leave early tomorrow.*
   Corrected: *We should leave early tomorrow.*

7. **Original:** *I can to help you with your homework.*
   Corrected: *I can help you with your homework.*

8. **Original:** *She needs to finish her project by tomorrow.*
   Corrected: *She needs to finish her project by tomorrow.* **(No correction needed)**

Split Infinitives

1. **Original:** *To thoroughly understand the topic, you need to study.*
   Corrected: *To understand the topic thoroughly, you need to study.*

2. **Original:** *To always be on time is important for success.*
   Corrected: *To be always on time is important for success.*

3. **Original:** *He tried to quietly leave the room.*
   Corrected: *He tried to leave the room quietly.*

4. **Original:** *To correctly solve the puzzle, focus on the clues.*
   Corrected: *To solve the puzzle correctly, focus on the clues.*

5. **Original:** *To effectively manage your time, create a schedule.*
   Corrected: *To manage your time effectively, create a schedule.*

6. **Original:** *To quickly answer the question, he raised his hand.*
   Corrected: *To answer the question quickly, he raised his hand.*

7. **Original:** *To clearly express your ideas, use simple language.*
   Corrected: *To express your ideas clearly, use simple language.*

8. **Original:** *To fully understand the concept, you must practice.*
   Corrected: *To understand the concept fully, you must practice.*

9

Hyphens

9.1   When to Use Hyphens

The correct use of hyphens can significantly impact the clarity of writing. This chapter covers the rules for using hyphens, particularly in compound modifiers, numbers, and other contexts where their placement can prevent ambiguity. Practical tips and exercises are provided to help writers master hyphen usage. §

Compound Modifiers

Figure 9.1: Hyphen (Vecteezy Library)

When two or more words work together as a single adjective before a noun, they should be hyphenated.

G. Grätzer, *The Little Book of Writing Better*,
https://doi.org/10.1007/978-3-031-76166-9_9

Examples:

Without hyphen:

A well known author shared her insights with the audience.

This could be misinterpreted as the author being both well and known, but not necessarily well-known as a single concept.

With hyphen:

A well-known author shared her insights with the audience.

But contrast this with:

The author's work is well known.

No hyphen is needed here because 'well' modifies 'known'.

Avoiding Ambiguity

Examples of potential ambiguity:

A "small business owner" could refer to a small business that is owned by someone, or it could imply a small person who owns a business.

Clearer:

A "small-business owner" clarifies that the person owns a small business.

Prefixes and Suffixes

Hyphens are often necessary with certain prefixes and suffixes to avoid confusion.

Re-sign vs. Resign 'Re-sign' means to sign again, while 'resign' means to quit.

> *After reviewing the contract, she decided to re-sign it with the updated terms.*

> *Frustrated with the new policies, the employee decided to resign.*

Re-cover vs. Recover 'Re-cover' means to cover something again, whereas 're-cover' means to regain something lost.

> *They decided to re-cover the sofa with new fabric.*

> *It took months for the economy to recover from the downturn.*

Like For example, 'shell-like' clarifies that something is similar to a shell.

> *The vase had a delicate, shell-like texture.*

> *The mineral's structure was similar to a shell in appearance.*

Many prefixes (e.g., 'non', 'multi', 'micro', 'semi') typically do not require a hyphen.

Examples:

'Nonprofit'—No hyphen is necessary.

'Multinational corporation'—No hyphen is necessary.

'Semi-independent'—Hyphen used for clarity; 'semiindependent' is difficult to read.

Numbers and Fractions

In writing, hyphens are used in compound numbers and fractions when written out in words.

For example, 'twenty-three' is used in compound numbers, and 'two-thirds' is used in fractions.

Avoiding Hyphens with Adverbs Ending in 'ly'

Adverbs ending in 'ly' do not require a hyphen when they modify an adjective before a noun.

Example:

A rapidly growing business.

A rapidly-growing business. (Incorrect use of hyphen)

9.2   Practice Makes Perfect

First Set

1. **Original:** "She is responsible of managing the team."
   Task: Correct the prepositional error in this sentence.
   Hint: *Consider the correct preposition that typically follows 'responsible'.*

2. **Original:** "He is interested for learning new skills."
   Task: Correct the prepositional error in this sentence.
   Hint: *Think about the common preposition that follows 'interested'.*

3. **Original:** "The book is different with what I expected."
   Task: Correct the prepositional error in this sentence.
   Hint: *Consider which preposition is commonly paired with 'different'.*

4. **Original:** "They are known as their honesty."
   Task: Correct the prepositional error in this sentence.
   Hint: *Think about the preposition that should follow 'known'.*

5. **Original:** "She is capable to solve complex problems."
   Task: Correct the prepositional error in this sentence.
   Hint: *Consider the preposition that typically follows 'capable'.*

6. **Original:** "He apologized of his mistake."
   Task: Correct the prepositional error in this sentence.
   Hint: *Think about the correct preposition that follows 'apologized'.*

7. **Original:** "The team is engaged to the project."
   Task: Correct the prepositional error in this sentence.
   Hint: *Consider the preposition that typically follows 'engaged'.*

8. **Original:** "She is confident to her abilities."
   Task: Correct the prepositional error in this sentence.
   Hint: What is the correct preposition to follow 'confident'?

Second Set

1. **Original:** "The decision was based of the evidence."
   Task: Correct the prepositional error in this sentence.
   Hint: Think about the proper preposition to use with 'based'.

2. **Original:** "He was accused for the crime."
   Task: Correct the prepositional error in this sentence.
   Hint: Consider which preposition is commonly used with 'accused'.

3. **Original:** "She is proud for her achievements."
   Task: Correct the prepositional error in this sentence.
   Hint: Consider which preposition typically follows 'proud'.

4. **Original:** "The project is dependent of external funding."
   Task: Correct the prepositional error in this sentence.
   Hint: Think about the preposition that typically follows 'dependent'.

5. **Original:** "They participated to the event."
   Task: Correct the prepositional error in this sentence.
   Hint: Consider the preposition that follows 'participated'.

6. **Original:** "The results are consistent to our expectations."
   Task: Correct the prepositional error in this sentence.
   Hint: Think about the preposition that typically follows 'consistent'.

7. **Original:** "She is accustomed with hard work."
   Task: Correct the prepositional error in this sentence.
   Hint: Consider the preposition that follows 'accustomed'.

8. **Original:** "He is proficient on using computers."
   Task: Correct the prepositional error in this sentence.
   Hint: Think about the correct preposition that follows 'proficient'.

Advanced

1. **Original:** "The contract is subject on approval."
   Task: Correct the prepositional error in this sentence.
   Hint: Consider which preposition typically follows 'subject'.

2. **Original:** "The company is liable of damages."
   Task: Correct the prepositional error in this sentence.
   Hint: Think about the preposition that should follow 'liable'.

3. **Original:** "She was concerned for her friend's health."
   Task: Correct the prepositional error in this sentence.
   Hint: Consider the preposition that typically follows 'concerned'.

4. **Original:** "He is committed with his goals."
   Task: Correct the prepositional error in this sentence.
   Hint: What is the correct preposition to follow 'committed'?

5. **Original:** "They were involved on the incident."
   Task: Correct the prepositional error in this sentence.
   Hint: Consider the preposition that typically follows 'involved'.

6. **Original:** "The decision is contingent in approval."
   Task: Correct the prepositional error in this sentence.
   Hint: Think about the preposition that typically follows 'contingent'.

7. **Original:** "The policy is aimed on improving safety."
   Task: Correct the prepositional error in this sentence.
   Hint: What is the correct preposition to follow 'aimed'?

8. **Original:** "He is interested to take part in the project."
   Task: Correct the prepositional error in this sentence.
   Hint: Consider the preposition that typically follows 'interested'.

9.3 PMP Solutions

First Set

1. **Solution:** "She is responsible for managing the team."
   Reason: The preposition 'of' was corrected to 'for' to properly follow 'responsible'.

2. **Solution:** "He is interested in learning new skills."
   Reason: The preposition 'for' was corrected to 'in' to properly follow 'interested'.

3. **Solution:** "The book is different from what I expected."
   Reason: The preposition 'with' was corrected to 'from' to properly follow 'different'.

4. **Solution:** "They are known for their honesty."
   Reason: The preposition 'as' was corrected to 'for' to properly follow 'known'.

5. **Solution:** "She is capable of solving complex problems."
   Reason: The preposition 'to' was corrected to 'of' to properly follow 'capable'.

6. **Solution:** "He apologized for his mistake."
   Reason: The preposition 'of' was corrected to 'for' to properly follow 'apologized'.

7. **Solution:** "The team is engaged in the project."
   Reason: The preposition 'to' was corrected to 'in' to properly follow 'engaged'.

8. **Solution:** "She is confident in her abilities."
   Reason: The preposition 'to' was corrected to 'in' to properly follow 'confident'.

Second Set

1. **Solution:** "The decision was based on the evidence."
   Reason: The preposition 'of' was corrected to 'on' to properly follow 'based'.

2. **Solution:** "He was accused of the crime."
   Reason: The preposition 'for' was corrected to 'of' to properly follow 'accused'.

3. **Solution:** "She is proud of her achievements."
   Reason: The preposition 'for' was corrected to 'of' to properly follow 'proud'.

4. **Solution:** "The project is dependent on external funding."
   Reason: The preposition 'of' was corrected to 'on' to properly follow 'dependent'.

5. **Solution:** "They participated in the event."
   Reason: The preposition 'to' was corrected to 'in' to properly follow 'participated'.

6. **Solution:** "The results are consistent with our expectations."
   Reason: The preposition 'to' was corrected to 'with' to properly follow 'consistent'.

7. **Solution:** "She is accustomed to hard work."
   Reason: The preposition 'with' was corrected to 'to' to properly follow 'accustomed'.

8. **Solution:** "He is proficient in using computers."
   Reason: The preposition 'on' was corrected to 'in' to properly follow 'proficient'.

Advanced

1. **Solution:** "The contract is subject to approval."
   Reason: The preposition 'on' was corrected to 'to' to properly follow 'subject'.

2. **Solution:** "The company is liable for damages."
   Reason: The preposition 'of' was corrected to 'for' to properly follow 'liable'.

3. **Solution:** "She was concerned about her friend's health."
   Reason: The preposition 'for' was corrected to 'about' to properly follow 'concerned'.

4. **Solution:** "He is committed to his goals."
   Reason: The preposition 'with' was corrected to 'to' to properly follow 'committed'.

5. **Solution:** "They were involved in the incident."
   Reason: The preposition 'on' was corrected to 'in' to properly follow 'involved'.

6. **Solution:** "The decision is contingent on approval."
   Reason: The preposition 'in' was corrected to 'on' to properly follow 'contingent'.

7. **Solution:** "The policy is aimed at improving safety."
   Reason: The preposition 'on' was corrected to 'at' to properly follow 'aimed'.

8. **Solution:** "He is interested in taking part in the project."
   Reason: The preposition 'to' was corrected to 'in' to properly follow 'interested'.

Direct vs. Indirect

This chapter compares direct and indirect speech, highlighting when each form should be used in writing. It also covers the rules for punctuating direct and indirect quotations and provides examples of how these structures can add variety and depth to writing. §

10.1 Introduction

This topic explores the characteristics, appropriate usage, and grammatical features of direct and indirect communication styles. It also provides practical guidance on how to convert between these styles, helping you navigate different communication contexts with ease.

10.2 Usage Contexts

When to Use Direct Communication

Direct communication is clear, concise, and straightforward. It is most appropriate in situations where clarity is paramount and there is no room for misinterpretation.

G. Grätzer, *The Little Book of Writing Better*,
https://doi.org/10.1007/978-3-031-76166-9_10

Direct communication is commonly used in the following contexts:

1. **Instructions:** When giving clear and unambiguous directions.
   Example: *Submit the report by 5 PM.*

2. **Commands:** When immediate action is required.
   Example: *Close the door.*

3. **Urgent Requests:** When a quick response is necessary.
   Example: *Call me immediately.*

When to Use Indirect Communication

In contrast, indirect communication is more nuanced and often used to convey messages in a polite or non-confrontational manner. It is useful in situations where maintaining harmony or showing respect is important:

1. **Requests:** To ask for something without being too forceful.
   Example: *Could you please submit the report by 5 PM?*

2. **Suggestions:** To propose ideas gently, leaving room for others' opinions.
   Example: *It might be a good idea to close the door.*

3. **Delicate Topics:** To address sensitive issues with care.
   Example: *Perhaps we should consider other options.*

10.3   Grammatical Features: Direct

Sentence Structure

Direct communication typically employs simple, straightforward sentence structures. Imperative and declarative sentences are common, with a clear subject-verb-object order. These sentences often lack modifiers, making them concise and to the point.

1. *Finish your work.*

2. *The meeting starts at 3 PM.*

Common Pitfalls

While direct communication is effective for clarity, it can sometimes come across as too blunt or even rude, especially if the context requires a more tactful approach. The lack of qualifiers or softening language can make statements seem overly harsh.
   Do this now. (This could be perceived as demanding rather than instructive.)

10.4   Grammatical Features: Indirect

Sentence Structure

Indirect communication often involves more complex sentence structures. It may include the passive voice, conditional clauses, or questions. The use of hedges, qualifiers, and modal verbs helps soften the message and convey politeness.

1. *It would be great if you could finish your work soon.*

2. *Perhaps the meeting should start at 3 PM?*

Common Pitfalls

The main issue with indirect communication is the potential for ambiguity. Overly vague or qualified statements can lead to misunderstandings, as the listener might not grasp the urgency or importance of the message.

> *Maybe we could start the meeting around 3 PM?* (This might leave the exact time unclear.)

10.5   Converting Between Direct and Indirect

Techniques for Conversion

Converting between direct and indirect communication involves making adjustments to tone, structure, and word choice. Here are some techniques to help you convert effectively:

1. **Adding or Removing Qualifiers:** Use words like *maybe*, *possibly*, or *could* to soften a direct statement, or remove them to make the message more direct.

2. **Changing Sentence Structure:** Convert imperative sentences to conditional or question forms.

3. **Modifying Tone with Modal Verbs:** Use modal verbs like *should*, *could*, or *would* to make a command sound like a suggestion.

Grammar Note: Verb Tense in Conversion

When converting direct communication to indirect communication, verb tense often shifts to reflect a change in perspective or time frame. In English, if the reporting verb (such as 'say' or 'ask') is in the past tense, the tense of the verb in the original direct speech typically shifts back in time:

- **Present Simple** in direct speech changes to **Past Simple** in indirect speech.
  - **Direct:** "I am tired."
  - **Indirect:** She said (that) she **was** tired.

- **Present Continuous** in direct speech changes to **Past Continuous** in indirect speech.

  - **Direct:** "I am working."

  - **Indirect:** He said (that) he **was working**.

- **Present Perfect** in direct speech changes to **Past Perfect** in indirect speech.

  - **Direct:** "I have finished my work."

  - **Indirect:** She said (that) she **had finished** her work.

This tense shift helps to maintain the sequence of events and ensures that the indirect statement accurately reflects the timing of the original direct statement.

10.6   Practice Makes Perfect

First Set

1. **Original:** "She is dependent of her parents for financial support."
   Task: Correct the prepositional error in this sentence.
   Hint: Consider the correct preposition that typically follows 'dependent'.

2. **Original:** "He is capable to handle multiple tasks."
   Task: Correct the prepositional error in this sentence.
   Hint: Think about the proper preposition that follows 'capable'.

3. **Original:** "The book is filled by interesting facts."
   Task: Correct the prepositional error in this sentence.
   Hint: Consider which preposition is commonly paired with 'filled'.

4. **Original:** "She is responsible of completing the project."
   Task: Correct the prepositional error in this sentence.
   Hint: Think about the correct preposition that follows 'responsible'.

5. **Original:** "He apologized about the mistake."
   Task: Correct the prepositional error in this sentence.
   Hint: Consider the preposition that is typically used with 'apologized'.

6. **Original:** "They are interested for learning new things."
   Task: Correct the prepositional error in this sentence.
   Hint: Think about the preposition that typically follows 'interested'.

7. **Original:** "The report is based of the survey results."
   Task: Correct the prepositional error in this sentence.
   Hint: Consider the correct preposition that follows 'based'.

8. **Original:** "She was accused for breaking the rules."
   Task: Correct the prepositional error in this sentence.
   Hint: What is the correct preposition to follow 'accused'?

Second Set

1. **Original:** "He is proficient on using various software programs."
   Task: Correct the prepositional error in this sentence.
   Hint: Consider the correct preposition that typically follows 'proficient'.

2. **Original:** "She is worried for the upcoming exam."
   Task: Correct the prepositional error in this sentence.
   Hint: Think about the preposition that typically follows 'worried'.

3. **Original:** "The document is consistent to the previous version."
   Task: Correct the prepositional error in this sentence.
   Hint: Consider the preposition that typically follows 'consistent'.

4. **Original:** "He succeeded on the first try."
   Task: Correct the prepositional error in this sentence.
   Hint: Think about the preposition that typically follows 'succeeded'.

5. **Original:** "The company is committed with providing quality services."
   Task: Correct the prepositional error in this sentence.
   Hint: Consider the correct preposition that typically follows 'committed'.

6. **Original:** "She is fluent on three languages."
   Task: Correct the prepositional error in this sentence.
   Hint: Think about the preposition that typically follows 'fluent'.

7. **Original:** "They participated to the event last week."
   Task: Correct the prepositional error in this sentence.
   Hint: Consider the correct preposition that typically follows 'participated'.

8. **Original:** "He is accustomed with the new schedule."
   Task: Correct the prepositional error in this sentence.
   Hint: What is the correct preposition to follow 'accustomed'?

Advanced

1. **Original:** "The outcome is contingent to the approval of the board."
   Task: Correct the prepositional error in this sentence.
   Hint: Consider the preposition that typically follows 'contingent'.

2. **Original:** "She is involved on several community projects."
   Task: Correct the prepositional error in this sentence.
   Hint: Think about the preposition that typically follows 'involved'.

3. **Original:** "The decision is dependent of external factors."
   Task: Correct the prepositional error in this sentence.
   Hint: Consider the preposition that typically follows 'dependent'.

4. **Original:** "He is known as his dedication to work."
   Task: Correct the prepositional error in this sentence.
   Hint: What is the correct preposition to follow 'known'?

5. **Original:** "The policy is aimed on reducing costs."
   Task: Correct the prepositional error in this sentence.
   Hint: Consider the preposition that typically follows 'aimed'.

6. **Original:** "She is concerned for the safety of the children."
   Task: Correct the prepositional error in this sentence.
   Hint: Think about the preposition that typically follows 'concerned'.

7. **Original:** "The team is reliant to the manager's guidance."
   Task: Correct the prepositional error in this sentence.
   Hint: Consider the preposition that typically follows 'reliant'.

8. **Original:** "He is proficient at using Excel."
   Task: Correct the prepositional error in this sentence.
   Hint: Think about the correct preposition that typically follows 'proficient'.

10.7   PMP Solutions

First Set

1. **Solution:** "She is dependent on her parents for financial support."
   Reason: The preposition 'of' was corrected to 'on' to properly follow 'dependent'.

2. **Solution:** "He is capable of handling multiple tasks."
   Reason: The preposition 'to' was corrected to 'of' to properly follow 'capable'.

3. **Solution:** "The book is filled with interesting facts."
   Reason: The preposition 'by' was corrected to 'with' to properly follow 'filled'.

4. **Solution:** "She is responsible for completing the project."
   Reason: The preposition 'of' was corrected to 'for' to properly follow 'responsible'.

5. **Solution:** "He apologized for the mistake."
   Reason: The preposition 'about' was corrected to 'for' to properly follow 'apologized'.

6. **Solution:** "They are interested in learning new things."
   Reason: The preposition 'for' was corrected to 'in' to properly follow 'interested'.

7. **Solution:** "The report is based on the survey results."
   Reason: The preposition 'of' was corrected to 'on' to properly follow 'based'.

8. **Solution:** "She was accused of breaking the rules."
   Reason: The preposition 'for' was corrected to 'of' to properly follow 'accused'.

Second Set

1. **Solution:** "He is proficient in using various software programs."
   Reason: The preposition 'on' was corrected to 'in' to properly follow 'proficient'.

2. **Solution:** "She is worried about the upcoming exam."
   Reason: The preposition 'for' was corrected to 'about' to properly follow 'worried'.

3. **Solution:** "The document is consistent with the previous version."
   Reason: The preposition 'to' was corrected to 'with' to properly follow 'consistent'.

4. **Solution:** "He succeeded in the first try."
   Reason: The preposition 'on' was corrected to 'in' to properly follow 'succeeded'.

5. **Solution:** "The company is committed to providing quality services."
   Reason: The preposition 'with' was corrected to 'to' to properly follow 'committed'.

6. **Solution:** "She is fluent in three languages."
   Reason: The preposition 'on' was corrected to 'in' to properly follow 'fluent'.

7. **Solution:** "They participatcd in the event last week."
   Reason: The preposition 'to' was corrected to 'in' to properly follow 'participated'.

8. **Solution:** "He is accustomed to the new schedule."
   Reason: The preposition 'with' was corrected to 'to' to properly follow 'accustomed'.

Advanced

1. **Solution:** "The outcome is contingent on the approval of the board."
   Reason: The preposition 'to' was corrected to 'on' to properly follow 'contingent'.

2. **Solution:** "She is involved in several community projects."
   Reason: The preposition 'on' was corrected to 'in' to properly follow 'involved'.

3. **Solution:** "The decision is dependent on external factors."
   Reason: The preposition 'of' was corrected to 'on' to properly follow 'dependent'.

4. **Solution:** "He is known for his dedication to work."
   Reason: The preposition 'as' was corrected to 'for' to properly follow 'known'.

5. **Solution:** "The policy is aimed at reducing costs."
   Reason: The preposition 'on' was corrected to 'at' to properly follow 'aimed'.

6. **Solution:** "She is concerned about the safety of the children."
   Reason: The preposition 'for' was corrected to 'about' to properly follow 'concerned'.

7. **Solution:** "The team is reliant on the manager's guidance."
   Reason: The preposition 'to' was corrected to 'on' to properly follow 'reliant'.

8. **Solution:** "He is proficient at using Excel." (Also, "He is proficient in using Excel.")
   Reason: The sentence is already correct, with 'at' being the appropriate preposition to follow 'proficient'.

Dashes

The en-dash and the em-dash are older siblings of the hyphen. Learn how to use en-dashes and em-dashes properly in writing. This chapter explains the functions of each type of dash, from setting off parenthetical information to indicating ranges or breaks in thought. With examples and exercises, readers will gain a thorough understanding of how dashes can add emphasis and clarity to their writing. **S**

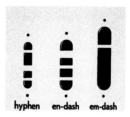

Figure 11.1: Dashes
(Vecteezy Library)

11.1 The En-Dash (–)

The en-dash is shorter than the em-dash yet longer than the hyphen. It is most commonly used to indicate ranges or connections. Think of it as a 'number dash'.

To Indicate Ranges

The en-dash connects a range of numbers, dates, or times, suggesting continuity between the values.

G. Grätzer, *The Little Book of Writing Better*,
https://doi.org/10.1007/978-3-031-76166-9_11

1. *It was published in vol. 25, pages 123–129.*

2. *The concert runs July 3–5.*

3. *Open from 10 AM–4 PM.*

4. *The event takes place 1990–2000.*

5. *The school year is from September–June.*

6. *The course is scheduled for 8 AM–12 PM.*

7. *Office hours are 9 AM–6 PM.*

8. *The exhibition runs from April 1–10.*

9. *Winter break is from December 20–January 2.*

To Connect Numbers, Words, or Names

The en-dash can connect items that are related or in contrast to each other, such as locations or names.

1. *The New York–London flight.*

2. *The author–editor relationship.*

3. *The team won 3–1.*

4. *The east–west divide is evident.*

5. *The doctor–patient confidentiality is crucial.*

6. *The Harvard–Yale rivalry is historic.*

7. *The north–south axis is strategic.*

8. *The manager–employee dynamic was positive.*

11.2   The Em-Dash (—)

The em-dash is longer than the en-dash and is used in several ways:

To Add Emphasis or an Interruption

Em-dashes replace commas, parentheses, or colons to add emphasis or introduce an interruption.

1. *My friend—the one who lives in Canada—is visiting next week.*

2. *She gave the best advice—don't give up.*

3. *The decision—which was unexpected—surprised everyone.*

4. *The meeting—scheduled for tomorrow—has been postponed.*

5. *The painting—a masterpiece—was stolen.*

6. *His plan—though risky—was approved.*

7. *The storm—which had been predicted—caused major damage.*

8. *The book—which I had read before—was fascinating.*

To Indicate Parenthetical Statements

Similar to parentheses, em-dashes enclose additional information.

1. *The book—which was a bestseller—was written in 2010.*

2. *Her idea—though unconventional—was brilliant.*

3. *The award—much deserved—was given to her.*

4. *The project—despite challenges—was successful.*

5. *The event—which was well-attended—raised funds for charity.*

6. *The discovery—made by accident—changed everything.*

7. *The car—a vintage model—was restored beautifully.*

8. *The film—which won several awards—was released last year.*

To Set Off Lists

An em-dash introduces a list or a restatement, offering a stylistic alternative to the colon.

1. *Three things are essential—patience, determination, and a positive attitude.*

2. *He packed everything—clothes, shoes, and his camera.*

3. *The recipe requires three ingredients—flour, sugar, and eggs.*

4. *The team focused on three areas—research, development, and marketing.*

5. *Her speech covered several topics—education, healthcare, and the environment.*

6. *The bag contained all the essentials—passport, wallet, and keys.*

7. *He was known for three traits—honesty, kindness, and wisdom.*

8. *The workshop focused on three skills—communication, leadership, and teamwork.*

11.3   When to Use Em-Dashes

Em-dashes are used to create a strong break in the structure of a sentence and are excellent for adding emphasis to the enclosed text.

1. *The truth—though hard to accept—is that we all make mistakes.*

2. *The decision—final and irrevocable—was announced yesterday.*

3. *The journey—long and arduous—was worth it.*

4. *The answer—simple yet profound—was correct.*

5. *The reality—harsh and unchanging—must be faced.*

6. *The plan—carefully crafted—was executed flawlessly.*

7. *The secret—known to few—was finally revealed.*

8. *The mission—dangerous but necessary—was a success.*

11.4   Parentheses for De-Emphasis

Parentheses are used to include additional information that is considered less important, providing extra details without detracting from the main point of the sentence.

1. *She bought a new car (a red one) last week.*

2. *The project was completed on time (despite some delays).*

3. *The book was a bestseller (according to the New York Times).*

4. *The test results (which were surprising) were discussed.*

5. *The dinner was delicious (especially the dessert).*

6. *He won the race (by a narrow margin).*

7. *The speech was impressive (considering the short notice).*

8. *The offer was accepted (much to everyone's surprise).*

11.5   Practice Makes Perfect

Set 1

1. The truth—though hard to accept—is that mistakes happen.
   Task: Identify and correct any issues with the use of em-dashes for emphasis in the sentence.
   Hint: Pay attention to the placement of the em-dashes around the emphasized clause.

2. She gave the best advice—keep going, no matter what.
   Task: Review the sentence for appropriate use of the em-dash.
   Hint: The em-dash should clearly introduce a key piece of advice.

3. John—exhausted from the journey—decided to rest before dinner.
   Task: Correct the sentence if the em-dashes are misplaced.
   Hint: Ensure that the em-dashes emphasize the middle clause correctly.

4. The decision—as difficult as it was—had to be made quickly.
   Task: Evaluate the em-dash usage for clarity and emphasis.
   Hint: Consider if the emphasis is on the difficult decision.

5. It was clear—from his tone—that he was upset.
   Task: Ensure proper usage of the em-dashes in this sentence.
   Hint: Focus on how the tone is emphasized.

6. The concert was amazing—the best one I've ever attended.
   Task: Correct any misuse of the em-dash.
   Hint: Does the em-dash appropriately highlight the key point?

7. She left early—not because she wanted to, but because she had no choice.
   Task: Check if the em-dashes emphasize the correct part of the sentence.
   Hint: Consider whether the reason for leaving is emphasized.

8. He made a promise—one that he intended to keep.
   Task: Assess the usage of the em-dash for emphasis.
   Hint: The em-dash should highlight the promise.

Set 2

1. The conference runs July 5–8.
   Task: Identify whether an en-dash or another punctuation mark is appropriate for the range in this sentence.
   Hint: Check if the en-dash properly connects a range of dates.

2. The meeting is scheduled from 9 AM–11 AM.
   Task: Confirm the proper use of the en-dash for time ranges.
   Hint: The en-dash is commonly used for time ranges.

3. The book covers the period 1850–1920 in great detail.
   Task: Ensure the correct use of the en-dash to indicate a time span.
   Hint: Is the range of years correctly connected with the en-dash?

4. The train journey takes 2–3 hours depending on traffic.
   Task: Review whether the en-dash is used correctly for the range.
   Hint: Verify if the en-dash is appropriate for the time range.

5. The reading covers pages 50–75 of the textbook.
   Task: Evaluate the use of the en-dash for the page range.
   Hint: Is the en-dash correctly used to represent a range of pages?

6. The store is open Monday–Friday.
   Task: Check if the en-dash is correctly applied for the range of days.
   Hint: Ensure that the range of days is properly connected by the en-dash.

7. The concert will run from 7–10 PM.
   Task: Review the time range and confirm the correct use of the en-dash.
   Hint: The en-dash should appropriately connect the start and end times.

8. The temperature fluctuated between 15–20 degrees Celsius.
   Task: Determine if the en-dash is correctly used for the temperature range.
   Hint: Check that the temperature range is connected with an en-dash.

11.6   PMP Solutions

Set 1

1. The truth—though hard to accept—is that mistakes happen.
   Solution: The em-dashes are correctly used to set off an emphasized clause in the middle of the sentence.

2. She gave the best advice—keep going, no matter what.
   Solution: The em-dash is used effectively to highlight the key piece of advice.

3. John—exhausted from the journey—decided to rest before dinner.
   Solution: The em-dashes are correctly placed to emphasize John's exhaustion from the journey.

4. The decision—as difficult as it was—had to be made quickly.
   Solution: The em-dashes properly emphasize the difficulty of the decision.

5. It was clear—from his tone—that he was upset.
   Solution: The em-dashes effectively emphasize the source of clarity (his tone).

6. The concert was amazing—the best one I've ever attended.
   Solution: The em-dash highlights the key point, which is that it was the best concert attended.

7. She left early—not because she wanted to, but because she had no choice.
   Solution: The em-dash properly emphasizes the explanation for her early departure.

8. He made a promise—one that he intended to keep.
   Solution: The em-dash correctly emphasizes the promise he made.

Set 2

1. The conference runs July 5–8.
   Solution: The en-dash is correctly used to indicate a range of dates.

2. The meeting is scheduled from 9 AM–11 AM.
   Solution: The en-dash is correctly used for the time range.

3. The book covers the period 1850–1920 in great detail.
   Solution: The en-dash is used correctly for the range of years.

4. The train journey takes 2–3 hours depending on traffic.
   Solution: The en-dash is correctly used for the time range of the journey.

5. The reading covers pages 50–75 of the textbook.
   Solution: The en-dash is properly used to indicate the range of pages.

6. The store is open Monday–Friday.
   Solution: The en-dash is correctly applied for the range of days.

7. The concert will run from 7–10 PM.
   Solution: The en-dash is used correctly to connect the time range for the concert.

8. The temperature fluctuated between 15–20 degrees Celsius.
   Solution: The en-dash is properly used to indicate the temperature range.

PART III

Important

Transitions: Longer Version

This expanded chapter delves deeper into the use of transitions, focusing on more nuanced forms that add sophistication to writing. Writers will learn how to use subtle transitions to create smoother and more engaging connections between ideas and paragraphs. §

Figure 12.1: Transition (Vecteezy Library)

© The Author(s), under exclusive license to Springer Nature Switzerland AG 2024
G. Grätzer, *The Little Book of Writing Better*,
https://doi.org/10.1007/978-3-031-76166-9_12

12.1   Types of Transition Words

There are six types of transition words and phrases.

1. Addition

Adds information or ideas.

- furthermore (emphasizes the strength of the argument)
    Eating healthy is important. Furthermore, *it helps in maintaining a good mood.*

- moreover (emphasizes the significance of the argument)
    Exercising regularly improves physical health. Moreover, *it boosts mental well-being.*

- in addition (more neutral term)
    Reading enhances knowledge. In addition, *it stimulates the mind.*

- also
    Writing is a form of expression. Also, *it helps improve communication skills.*

2. Comparison and Contrast

Signals differences—or similarities—between ideas.

- however (introduces a statement that contrasts with an earlier statement)
    Cats are independent animals. However, *dogs are more social.*

- on the other hand (considering an alternative perspective)
    Summer is hot and sunny. On the other hand, *winter is cold and snowy.*

- by contrast and in contrast (directly compare two or more items; stronger than 'however' in emphasizing difference)
    A professional athlete trains daily. By contrast, *a hobbyist might only exercise occasionally.*

Figure 12.2: Comparison and contrast (Vecteezy Library)

- similarly (indicates likeness)
    Brushing your teeth keeps them clean. Similarly, *flossing helps maintain dental health.*

3. Cause and Effect

Shows the relationship: condition and outcome.

- therefore (direct conclusion)
    She studied hard for the exam. Therefore, *she passed with high marks.*

- thus (similar to 'therefore', but implies a softer transition)
    He followed the recipe exactly. Thus, *the cake turned out perfect.*

- as a result (explicitly attributes a consequence of the preceding facts)
    She saved money every month. As a result, *she was able to buy a new car.*

- consequently (a cause-and-effect relationship)
    He skipped breakfast. Consequently, *he felt hungry before lunch.*

4. Sequence and Order

Organizes information chronologically or logically.

- the words 'first', 'next', 'then', and 'finally' are used to organize steps in an argument.
    First, *gather all the ingredients.* Next, *mix them together.* Then, *bake the mixture in the oven.* Finally, *let it cool before serving.*

- The sequence of words: 'initially', 'subsequently', 'meanwhile', 'finally' indicate the steps in a process.
    Initially, *start by creating an outline for your essay.* Subsequently, *write the introduction.* Meanwhile, *gather your thoughts for the body paragraphs.* Finally, *conclude with a strong closing statement.*

- 'before', 'after', 'during' signify events relative to each other in time.
    Wash your hands before *eating.*
    After *dinner, go for a walk.*
    During *the presentation, take notes to help with the discussion.*

- 'Next', 'then', 'later' indicate the immediate sequence or logical progression in actions, steps, or events.
    Next, *prepare your notes for the meeting.*
    Then, *review the agenda to ensure you're ready.*
    Later, *you can follow up on any unresolved points.*

- 'meanwhile', 'concurrently' describe simultaneous events.
    She was preparing the meal; meanwhile, *her friend set the table.*
    The team worked on the project; concurrently, *they also prepared the presentation.*

5. Emphasis

Words (and the phrase) such as 'indeed', 'in fact', and 'notably' highlight key points.

- indeed (strengthening the statement that precedes it)

- in fact (introduces a piece of evidence or an example that supports the claim)

- most importantly (the most significant point)
    Indeed, *getting regular exercise is crucial for overall health.*
    In fact, *studies show that regular exercise can improve mood and reduce stress.*
    Most importantly, *regular physical activity can help prevent chronic diseases.*

6. Summary and Conclusion

- in summary (introduces a summary)

- to sum up (similar to the previous one)

- in conclusion (a strong closing statement or a concise summary of findings)
    In summary, *adopting a healthy lifestyle can lead to a longer, happier life.*
    To sum up, *making small changes in your daily routine can have a big impact on your health.*
    In conclusion, *the benefits of regular exercise, a balanced diet, and adequate rest cannot be overstated.*

The transition words listed in the categories are examples, not complete lists. To illustrate, here are some *common* transition words and phrases in the Addition category:

and	additionally
also	again
moreover	too
furthermore	plus
in addition	indeed
besides	in fact
likewise	of course
as well as	then
not only… but also	equally important
equally	furthermore
similarly	more importantly

12.2   Practice Makes Perfect

Set 1

1. Identify the transition word in this sentence and explain its purpose: "She was tired; nevertheless, she continued to work."
   Hint: Look for a word that connects contrasting ideas.

2. Rewrite the following sentence using a transition that indicates a sequence: "She woke up. She made breakfast."
   Hint: Think about transition words that show the order of events.

3. Choose an appropriate transition word to fill in the blank: "She wanted to go for a walk.____ , it started raining." (Options: However, Therefore, Meanwhile.)
   Hint: Consider the relationship between the two events.

4. Identify and correct the misplaced transition in the following sentence: "She arrived late. Nonetheless, the meeting had already ended, thus."
   Hint: Consider the logical flow of ideas and the proper placement of transitions.

5. Use a transition word to combine the following sentences into one: "The presentation was informative. It was too long."
   Hint: Think about transition words that indicate a contrast.

6. Which transition word would best complete the sentence? "He practiced every day;____ , he improved his skills." (Options: Consequently, However, Moreover.)
   Hint: Look for a transition that shows cause and effect.

7. Identify the type of transition used in the following sentence: "Lastly, we need to review the final draft."
   Hint: Think about the transition's role in indicating the order of actions.

8. Rewrite the following sentence using a transition that shows an addition of information: "She finished her homework. She also helped her brother with his."
   Hint: Consider transition words that indicate additional information.

Set 2

1. Identify the transition word in this sentence and explain its purpose: "He didn't understand the topic; therefore, he asked for help."
   Hint: Look for a word that shows cause and effect.

2. Rewrite the following sentence using a transition that indicates a result: "She studied hard. She passed the exam."
   Hint: Think about transition words that show one event leading to another.

3. Choose an appropriate transition word to fill in the blank: "He was hungry.____ , he went to the kitchen." (Options: Subsequently, Nevertheless, For example.)
   Hint: Consider how the second event follows from the first.

4. Identify and correct the misplaced transition in the following sentence: "The project was completed on time. In addition, it was under budget, finally."
   Hint: Consider the logical sequence and where the transition should be placed.

5. Use a transition word to combine the following sentences into one: "She wanted to join the team. She had to improve her skills first."

Hint: Think about transition words that indicate a condition.

6. Which transition word would best complete the sentence?
   "He missed the bus;____ , he had to walk to work." (Options: Thus, In contrast, Similarly.)
   Hint: Look for a transition that indicates a consequence.

7. Identify the type of transition used in the following sentence: "On the other hand, the new policy could have negative consequences."
   Hint: Think about the transition's role in contrasting ideas.

8. Rewrite the following sentence using a transition that shows an example: "Many students find this concept difficult. This concept is not easy."
   Hint: Consider transition words that introduce an example.

12.3   PMP Solutions

Set 1 Solutions

1. Transition word: 'Nevertheless' indicates a contrast between being tired and continuing to work.

2. Rewritten sentence: "She woke up, and then she made breakfast."

3. Correct choice: 'However'. "She wanted to go for a walk. However, it started raining."

4. Corrected sentence: "She arrived late. Nonetheless, the meeting had already ended."

5. Combined sentence: "The presentation was informative; however, it was too long."

6. Best choice: 'Consequently'. "He practiced every day; consequently, he improved his skills."

7. Type of transition: 'Lastly' is a transition used for indicating the order of actions.

8. Rewritten sentence: "She finished her homework, and in addition, she helped her brother with his."

Set 2 Solutions

1. Transition word: 'Therefore' indicates a cause-and-effect relationship between not understanding the topic and asking for help.

2. Rewritten sentence: "She studied hard; as a result, she passed the exam."

3. Correct choice: 'Subsequently'. "He was hungry. Subsequently, he went to the

kitchen."

4. Corrected sentence: "The project was completed on time. Finally, it was under budget."

5. Combined sentence: "She wanted to join the team, but she had to improve her skills first."

6. Best choice: 'Thus'. "He missed the bus; thus, he had to walk to work."

7. Type of transition: "On the other hand" is a transition used for contrasting ideas.

8. Rewritten sentence: "Many students find this concept difficult; for instance, this concept is not easy."

Run-on Sentences

Run-on sentences can make writing difficult to follow and disrupt the flow of ideas. This chapter explains how to identify and fix run-on sentences, offering strategies to break them into clear, concise, and properly structured sentences. 🅂

A 'run-on sentence' occurs when two or more sentences, or rather, clauses, are improperly connected without appropriate punctuation or conjunctions. Run-on sentences often make the text difficult to follow and can confuse the reader.

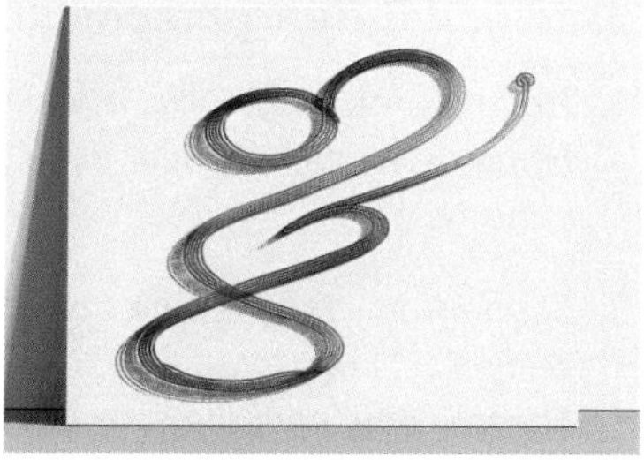

13.1   Examples

Traditional Examples

Figure 13.1: Run-on sentences
(Vecteezy Library)

I love to write, it is my passion, I spend hours every day at my desk writing stories, none of them are published yet. 😣

Corrected: *I love to write; it is my passion. I spend hours every day at my desk writing stories, but none of them are published yet.* 🙂

Improper Sequence Without Separation

I finished my homework I went to the park I played with my friends. 😣
   Corrected: *I finished my homework, I went to the park, and I played with my friends.* 😊

Concepts Without Proper Segmentation

The Earth revolves around the Sun the Moon revolves around the Earth the Solar System is part of the Milky Way Galaxy. 😣
   Corrected: *The Earth revolves around the Sun. The Moon revolves around the Earth. The Solar System is part of the Milky Way Galaxy.* 😊

13.2   Avoiding Run-on Sentences

To avoid run-on sentences in your writing, you can:

1. Use punctuation such as periods (.) or semicolons (;) to separate independent clauses.

2. Use coordinating conjunctions (for, and, nor, but, or, yet, so) with a comma to connect independent clauses.

3. Break complex ideas into simpler, more digestible sentences.

13.3   Practice Makes Perfect

For each of the following sentences, identify and correct the run-on sentences. Use appropriate punctuation, conjunctions, or sentence segmentation.

Traditional Run-on Sentences

1. *He loves reading he has a huge collection of books.*
   Hint: *Consider where to place periods or semicolons to separate the independent clauses.*

2. *She enjoys cooking she spends hours in the kitchen experimenting with new recipes.*
   Hint: *Think about how to break this into two separate sentences.*

3. *The cat chased the mouse the mouse ran under the sofa.*
   Hint: *Identify the two independent actions and separate them.*

4. *I was tired I decided to take a nap.*
   Hint: *Use punctuation or conjunctions to separate these two ideas.*

5. *The sun was shining the birds were singing.*
   Hint: *Consider adding a conjunction or punctuation to separate the two ideas.*

6. *She likes ice cream he prefers cake.*
   Hint: *How can you properly separate these contrasting preferences?*

7. *We went shopping we bought a lot of clothes.*
   Hint: *Identify the point where the sentence can be divided.*

8. *The project was difficult we managed to finish it on time.*
   Hint: *Consider how to use punctuation to clarify the sentence.*

Improper Sequence Without Separation

1. *I woke up I brushed my teeth I had breakfast.*
   Hint: *How can you properly separate these sequential events?*

2. *He opened the door he stepped outside he took a deep breath.*
   Hint: *Look for logical breaks between actions.*

3. *We packed our bags we headed to the airport we caught our flight.*
   Hint: *Use appropriate punctuation to separate the events.*

4. *She finished her homework she went to the park she played with her friends.*
   Hint: *Consider how to make this sequence clearer.*

5. *The sun set we lit the campfire we started cooking.*
   Hint: *Break down the actions into separate events.*

6. *The alarm rang I woke up I got ready for work.*
   Hint: *How can you clarify the sequence of actions?*

7. *The dog barked the cat ran away the bird flew off.*
   Hint: *Consider using punctuation to improve readability.*

8. *The train arrived we got on board we found our seats.*
   Hint: *Think about where to place punctuation to separate the actions.*

Concepts Without Proper Segmentation

1. *The Earth orbits the Sun the Moon orbits the Earth.*
   Hint: *Break down the sentence into separate, related thoughts.*

2. *Electricity powers our homes water flows through our pipes.*
   Hint: *Separate the concepts for clarity.*

3. *The brain controls the body the heart pumps blood.*
   Hint: *Identify the two distinct ideas and separate them.*

4. *Photosynthesis occurs in plants respiration occurs in animals.*
   Hint: *Consider using punctuation to distinguish these two processes.*

5. *Computers process data phones connect people.*
   Hint: *Separate the two distinct functions.*

6. *The engine powers the car the wheels move it forward.*
   Hint: *Identify the different functions and separate them.*

7. *The teacher explains the lesson the students take notes.*
   Hint: *Consider adding punctuation to separate the actions.*

8. *The sun provides light the moon reflects it.*
   Hint: *Think about how to separate these related concepts.*

Run-on with Conjunction Misuse

1. *The rain was heavy it was difficult to see, and I was getting soaked.*
   Hint: *Consider where to add punctuation to separate the two independent clauses properly.*

2. *The cake was delicious it was chocolate, and everyone loved it.*
   Hint: *Think about how to correctly use conjunctions and punctuation.*

3. *The movie was long it was entertaining, and we stayed until the end.*
   Hint: *Separate the ideas and use proper conjunctions.*

4. *The sun was shining it was a perfect day, and we decided to go to the beach.*
   Hint: *Consider using punctuation to improve sentence clarity.*

5. *The team worked hard it was a challenging project, and they completed it on time.*
   Hint: *Identify where punctuation or conjunctions are needed.*

6. *The car was old it was still reliable, and we drove it across the country.*
   Hint: *Break down the sentence for clarity using punctuation.*

7. *The book was interesting it was full of detailed information, and I learned a lot from it.*
   Hint: *Consider the proper use of conjunctions and punctuation.*

8. *The dinner was delicious it was well-prepared, and everyone enjoyed it.*
   Hint: *Add punctuation to separate the clauses correctly.*

13.4   PMP Solutions

Traditional Run-on Sentences

1. **Original:** *He loves reading he has a huge collection of books.*
   Corrected: *He loves reading; he has a huge collection of books.*

2. **Original:** *She enjoys cooking she spends hours in the kitchen experimenting with new recipes.*
   Corrected: *She enjoys cooking. She spends hours in the kitchen experimenting with new recipes.*

3. **Original:** *The cat chased the mouse the mouse ran under the sofa.*
   Corrected: *The cat chased the mouse; the mouse ran under the sofa.*

4. **Original:** *I was tired I decided to take a nap.*
   Corrected: *I was tired, so I decided to take a nap.*

5. **Original:** *The sun was shining the birds were singing.*
   Corrected: *The sun was shining, and the birds were singing.*

6. **Original:** *She likes ice cream he prefers cake.*
   Corrected: *She likes ice cream, but he prefers cake.*

7. **Original:** *We went shopping we bought a lot of clothes.*
   Corrected: *We went shopping, and we bought a lot of clothes.*

8. **Original:** *The project was difficult we managed to finish it on time.*
   Corrected: *The project was difficult, but we managed to finish it on time.*

Improper Sequence Without Separation

1. **Original:** *I woke up I brushed my teeth I had breakfast.*
   Corrected: *I woke up, brushed my teeth, and had breakfast.*

2. **Original:** *He opened the door he stepped outside he took a deep breath.*
   Corrected: *He opened the door, stepped outside, and took a deep breath.*

3. **Original:** *We packed our bags we headed to the airport we caught our flight.*
   Corrected: *We packed our bags, headed to the airport, and caught our flight.*

4. **Original:** *She finished her homework she went to the park she played with her friends.*
   Corrected: *She finished her homework, went to the park, and played with her friends.* Alternative: *After she finished her homework, she went to the park and played with her friends.*

5. **Original:** *The sun set we lit the campfire we started cooking.*
   Corrected: *The sun set, we lit the campfire, and we started cooking.*

6. **Original:** *The alarm rang I woke up I got ready for work.*
   Corrected: *The alarm rang, I woke up, and I got ready for work.*

7. **Original:** *The dog barked the cat ran away the bird flew off.*
   Corrected: *The dog barked, the cat ran away, and the bird flew off.*

8. **Original:** *The train arrived we got on board we found our seats.*
   Corrected: *The train arrived, we got on board, and we found our seats.*

Concepts Without Proper Segmentation

1. **Original:** *The Earth orbits the Sun the Moon orbits the Earth.*
   Corrected: *The Earth orbits the Sun. The Moon orbits the Earth.*

2. **Original:** *Electricity powers our homes water flows through our pipes.*
   Corrected: *Electricity powers our homes. Water flows through our pipes.*

3. **Original:** *The brain controls the body the heart pumps blood.*
   Corrected: *The brain controls the body. The heart pumps blood.*

4. **Original:** *Photosynthesis occurs in plants respiration occurs in animals.*
   Corrected: *Photosynthesis occurs in plants. Respiration occurs in animals.*

5. **Original:** *Computers process data phones connect people.*
   Corrected: *Computers process data. Phones connect people.*

6. **Original:** *The engine powers the car the wheels move it forward.*
   Corrected: *The engine powers the car. The wheels move it forward.*

7. **Original:** *The teacher explains the lesson the students take notes.*
   Corrected: *The teacher explains the lesson. The students take notes.*

8. **Original:** *The sun provides light the moon reflects it.*
   Corrected: *The sun provides light. The moon reflects it.*

Run-on with Conjunction Misuse

1. **Original:** *The rain was heavy it was difficult to see, and I was getting soaked.*
   Corrected: *The rain was heavy; it was difficult to see, and I was getting soaked.*

2. **Original:** *The cake was delicious it was chocolate, and everyone loved it.*
   Corrected: *The cake was delicious; it was chocolate, and everyone loved it.*

3. **Original:** *The movie was long it was entertaining, and we stayed until the end.*
   Corrected: *The movie was long, but it was entertaining, and we stayed until the end.*

4. **Original:** *The sun was shining it was a perfect day, and we decided to go to the beach.*
   Corrected: *The sun was shining; it was a perfect day, and we decided to go to the beach.*

5. **Original:** *The team worked hard it was a challenging project, and they completed it on time.*
   Corrected: *The team worked hard; it was a challenging project, and they completed it on time.*

6. **Original:** *The car was old it was still reliable, and we drove it across the country.*
   Corrected: *The car was old, but it was still reliable, and we drove it across the country.*

7. **Original:** *The book was interesting it was full of detailed information, and I learned a lot from it.*
   Corrected: *The book was interesting; it was full of detailed information, and I learned a lot from it.*

8. **Original:** *The dinner was delicious it was well-prepared, and everyone enjoyed it.*
   Corrected: *The dinner was delicious; it was well-prepared, and everyone enjoyed it.*

14

Only

The placement of 'only' can drastically change the meaning of a sentence. This chapter provides detailed guidance on where to place it in different sentence structures to ensure clarity and avoid ambiguity.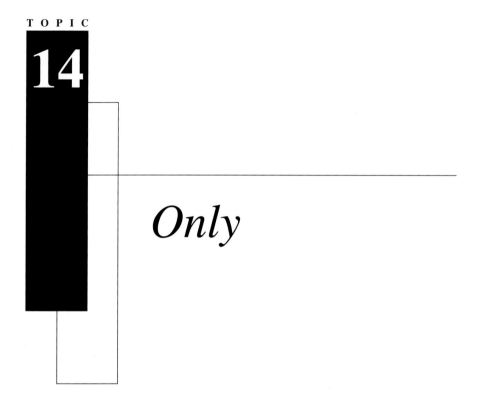

"Only the Lonely" (Know the Way I Feel) is a 1960 song written by Roy Orbison and Joe Melson.

Figure 14.1: Only the Lonely (Vecteezy Library)

© The Author(s), under exclusive license to Springer Nature Switzerland AG 2024   117
G. Grätzer, *The Little Book of Writing Better*,
https://doi.org/10.1007/978-3-031-76166-9_14

Such a simple word: 'only'. Yet its placement can dramatically alter the meaning of a sentence.

'Only' is an adverb used to signify that something is limited to a specific case mentioned; nothing else applies. The placement of 'only' is crucial as it defines the scope of a statement, the uniqueness of a situation, or the specific conditions under which a statement holds true.

14.1   Placement of 'Only'

Only Before the Verb

When 'only' precedes a verb, it restricts the action to the condition or object that follows.

John only has five apples. 😊
In this sentence, 'only' indicates that John possesses no more than five apples.

Only Before the Subject

Placing 'only' immediately before the subject emphasizes exclusivity.
The only cars available are electric. 😊
This sentence emphasizes that exclusively electric cars are available.

Only Before the Object

When 'only' precedes the object, it limits the statement exclusively to that object.
The sale applies to in-store purchases only. 😊
This indicates that the sale is not applicable to online purchases.

14.2   Misplacing 'Only'

Misplacing 'only' can subtly change the meaning of a statement, leading to confusion.

Correct: *Only the employees who worked overtime received bonuses.* 😊
Meaning: Bonuses were given exclusively to employees who worked overtime.

Incorrect: *The employees who only worked overtime received bonuses.* 😣
Meaning: The employees did nothing but work overtime, which is unlikely the intended message.

14.3   More Illustrations

1. *Only students in the advanced class can solve this problem in under an hour.* 😊
   Meaning: Exclusively students in the advanced class can solve the problem in under an hour.

2. *The teacher only explained the main concepts in the last lecture.* 😊
   Meaning: The teacher did nothing but explain the main concepts during the last lecture.

3. *Only when the conditions are met can the experiment begin.* 😊
   Meaning: The experiment can only begin if the conditions are met.

4. *The test results only affect the final grade slightly.* 😊
   Meaning: The test results have a slight impact on the final grade.

14.4 Practice Makes Perfect

Only Before the Verb

1. *She only speaks French.*
   Hint: *Think about what language she speaks and whether anything else is implied.*

2. *They only visit during the holidays.*
   Hint: *Consider what time frame their visits are limited to.*

3. *He only drives on weekends.*
   Hint: *Focus on when he drives. Is it limited to a specific time?*

4. *The company only sells organic products.*
   Hint: *What type of products does the company sell? Is it exclusive?*

5. *He only reads non-fiction.*
   Hint: *Consider what genre of books he reads. Is there any limitation?*

6. *She only eats vegetarian food.*
   Hint: *Think about what type of food she eats. Is it restricted to something specific?*

7. *They only accept cash payments.*
   Hint: *What form of payment is accepted? Is it exclusive?*

8. *The dog only barks at strangers.*
   Hint: *Who does the dog bark at? Is it limited to a specific group?*

Only Before the Subject

1. *Only the manager can approve this request.*
   Hint: *Who is the only person with the authority to approve the request?*

2. *Only John and Mary were present at the meeting.*
   Hint: *Who were the exclusive attendees of the meeting?*

3. *Only the main characters survived the disaster.*

Hint: Who survived the disaster? Is it limited to certain characters?

4. *Only experienced hikers should attempt this trail.*
   Hint: Who is the trail intended for? Consider the experience level.

5. *Only the CEO can authorize this decision.*
   Hint: Who has the exclusive authority to authorize the decision?

6. *Only the authorized personnel have access to this area.*
   Hint: Who is allowed access to this area? Is it limited to certain people?

7. *Only seniors are eligible for this discount.*
   Hint: Who qualifies for the discount? Is it limited by age or group?

8. *Only the top students received awards.*
   Hint: Who received awards? Was it an exclusive group?

Only Before the Object

1. *The discount applies to selected items only.*
   Hint: What is the discount limited to? Is it applicable to everything or specific items?

2. *He accepts cash payments only.*
   Hint: What type of payment is accepted? Is it restricted?

3. *The service is available to members only.*
   Hint: Who can avail of the service? Is it limited to a specific group?

4. *The invitation is for guests only.*
   Hint: Who is the invitation intended for? Is it restricted to certain people?

5. *The product is for internal use only.*
   Hint: Where can the product be used? Is it limited to a specific setting?

6. *The offer is valid for a limited time only.*
   Hint: How long is the offer available? Is it time-restricted?

7. *This road is for residents only.*
   Hint: Who is allowed to use the road? Is it open to everyone?

8. *The class is open to beginners only.*
   Hint: Who can join the class? Is it limited to a specific skill level?

Misplacing 'Only'

1. *The employees who only worked weekends received bonuses.*
   Hint: Does this imply that working on weekends was their only task?

2. *Students who only study hard will succeed.*
   Hint: *Does this suggest that studying hard is the only factor in their success?*

3. *He only watches documentaries.*
   Hint: *Is his viewing limited to documentaries? Does it exclude other genres?*

4. *She only brought her laptop.*
   Hint: *What does this imply about what she brought? Was anything else included?*

5. *They only offered a refund to members.*
   Hint: *Was the refund exclusive to members, or does this imply something else?*

6. *We only discussed the main topics.*
   Hint: *What topics were discussed? Was the discussion limited to specific areas?*

7. *He only eats vegetables.*
   Hint: *Is his diet limited to vegetables, or does this imply something else?*

8. *She only spoke about the first chapter.*
   Hint: *Was her discussion limited to the first chapter, or does this suggest more?*

More Illustrations

1. *The company only offers health benefits to full-time employees.*
   Hint: *Who are the health benefits offered to? Is it limited to a specific group?*

2. *The report only covers the last quarter.*
   Hint: *What time period does the report cover? Is it restricted?*

3. *The teacher only reviews the most important concepts before the exam.*
   Hint: *What does the teacher focus on during the review? Is it selective?*

4. *The membership is only available to gold members.*
   Hint: *Who can access the membership? Is it limited to a certain level?*

5. *The update is only compatible with the latest version.*
   Hint: *What does the update work with? Is it restricted to specific versions?*

6. *The course only includes online materials.*
   Hint: *What type of materials are included in the course? Are there any other types?*

7. *The promotion is only valid for new customers.*
   Hint: *Who can benefit from the promotion? Is it limited to certain customers?*

8. *The store only stocks eco-friendly products.*
   Hint: *What type of products are available in the store? Is there a specific focus?*

Only and Ambiguity

1. *The package only includes a manual and a charger.*
   Hint: *What does the package include? Is there ambiguity in what is covered?*

2. *She only answered the last question correctly.*
   Hint: *Did she answer other questions? How does 'only' affect the interpretation?*

3. *Only the supervisor can sign this document.*
   Hint: *Who has the authority to sign the document? Is it exclusive?*

4. *He only managed to solve two problems.*
   Hint: *How many problems did he solve? Is there a limitation implied?*

5. *The contract only covers damages caused by accidents.*
   Hint: *What type of damages are covered? Is it limited to specific circumstances?*

6. *The scholarship is only for undergraduate students.*
   Hint: *Who is eligible for the scholarship? Is it restricted to a specific group?*

7. *She only wore black to the event.*
   Hint: *What color did she wear? Does 'only' imply something about her choice?*

8. *The warranty only applies to manufacturing defects.*
   Hint: *What does the warranty cover? Is it limited to specific issues?*

Only and Implication

1. *The warranty only covers manufacturing defects.*
   Hint: *What does the warranty cover? Is it limited to manufacturing defects?*

2. *They hired only two new employees.*
   Hint: *How many employees were hired? Is this a small or expected number?*

3. *He reads only fiction.*
   Hint: *What type of books does he read? Is it limited to a specific genre?*

4. *The offer applies to only online purchases.*
   Hint: *Where is the offer valid? Is it limited to a specific purchase method?*

5. *The project required only minimal resources.*
   Hint: *How much was needed for the project? Does 'only' downplay the effort?*

6. *The policy changed only last year.*
   Hint: *When did the policy change? Is this a recent change?*

7. *They visited only the main attractions.*
   Hint: *What did they visit? Were other places skipped?*

8. *She uses only organic skincare products.*
    Hint: *What type of products does she use? Is there a preference implied?*

Only and Nuance

1. *The offer is available for only a limited time.*
    Hint: *How long is the offer available? Is there a sense of urgency implied?*

2. *She needs to pass only one more exam to graduate.*
    Hint: *How many exams does she need to pass? Is this the final step?*

3. *They want only a simple solution.*
    Hint: *What type of solution do they want? Is it limited in complexity?*

4. *He asked for only a brief meeting.*
    Hint: *What type of meeting did he request? Does 'only' suggest a short duration?*

5. *The job requires only basic computer skills.*
    Hint: *What skills are needed for the job? Is it limited to basic skills?*

6. *The app works on only Android devices.*
    Hint: *What devices are compatible with the app? Is there a limitation?*

7. *They planned only a short trip.*
    Hint: *How long is the trip? Is it shorter than usual?*

8. *She requested only a small favor.*
    Hint: *What did she ask for? Is it something minor?*

14.5   PMP Solutions

Only Before the Verb

1. *She speaks* only *French.*

2. *They visit* only *during the holidays.*

3. *He drives* only *on weekends.*

4. *The company sells* only *organic products.*

5. *He reads* only *non-fiction.*

6. *She eats* only *vegetarian food.*

7. *They accept* only *cash payments.*

8. *The dog barks* only *at strangers.*

Only Before the Subject

1. Only *the manager can approve this request.*

2. Only *John and Mary were present at the meeting.*

3. Only *the main characters survived the disaster.*

4. Only *experienced hikers should attempt this trail.*

5. Only *the CEO can authorize this decision.*

6. Only *the authorized personnel have access to this area.*

7. Only *seniors are eligible for this discount.*

8. Only *the top students received awards.*

Only Before the Object

1. *The discount applies to* selected items only.

2. *He accepts* cash payments only.

3. *The service is available to* members only.

4. *The invitation is for* guests only.

5. *The product is for* internal use only.

6. *The offer is valid for* a limited time only.

7. *This road is for* residents only.

8. *The class is open to* beginners only.

Misplacing 'Only'

1. *The employees who worked* only *weekends received bonuses.*

2. *Students who study* only *hard will succeed.*

3. *He watches* only *documentaries.*

4. *She brought* only *her laptop.*

5. *They offered a refund to* only *members.*

6. *We discussed* only *the main topics.*

7. *He eats* only *vegetables.*

8. *She spoke about* only *the first chapter.*

More Illustrations

1. *The company offers* only *health benefits to full-time employees.*

2. *The report covers* only *the last quarter.*

3. *The teacher reviews* only *the most important concepts before the exam.*

4. *The membership is available to* only *gold members.*

5. *The update is compatible with* only *the latest version.*

6. *The course includes* only *online materials.*

7. *The promotion is valid for* only *new customers.* (Alternatives: *The promotion is valid* only *for new customers. The promotion is valid for new customers* only.)

8. *The store stocks* only *eco-friendly products.*

Only and Ambiguity

1. *The package includes* only *a manual and a charger.*

2. *She answered* only *the last question correctly.*

3. Only *the supervisor can sign this document.*

4. *He managed to solve* only *two problems.*

5. *The contract covers* only *damages caused by accidents.*

6. *The scholarship is for* only *undergraduate students.*

7. *She wore* only *black to the event.*

8. *The warranty applies to* only *manufacturing defects.*

Only and Implication

1. *The warranty covers* only *manufacturing defects.*

2. *They hired* only *two new employees.*

3. *He reads* only *fiction.*

4. *The offer applies to* only *online purchases.*

5. *The project required* only *minimal resources.*

6. *The policy changed* only *last year.*

7. *They visited* only *the main attractions.*

8. *She uses* only *organic skincare products.*

Only and Nuance

1. *The offer is available for* only *a limited time.*

2. *She needs to pass* only *one more exam to graduate.*

3. *They want* only *a simple solution.*

4. *He asked for* only *a brief meeting.*

5. *The job requires* only *basic computer skills.*

6. *The app works on* only *Android devices.*

7. *They planned* only *a short trip.*

8. *She requested* only *a small favor.*

Comma Before If

Commas can change the meaning of a sentence, particularly before conditional clauses. This chapter explains the rules for placing commas before 'if' and other conditional words, helping writers to avoid common pitfalls in their writing. §

Figure 15.1: Dependent Klaus (Vecteezy Library)

15.1 Dependent and Independent Clauses

To correctly understand and apply the use of commas in sentences involving dependent and independent clauses, especially with conditional sentences and conjunctions, let's clarify these concepts with examples and explanations.

© The Author(s), under exclusive license to Springer Nature Switzerland AG 2024   127
G. Grätzer, *The Little Book of Writing Better*,
https://doi.org/10.1007/978-3-031-76166-9_15

Understanding Dependent and Independent Clauses

An 'independent clause' is a group of words that contains a subject and verb and expresses a complete thought. It can stand alone as a sentence. A 'dependent clause' cannot stand alone as a sentence because it does not express a complete thought. It usually provides additional information to an independent clause and is often introduced by conjunctions like 'if', 'because', 'although', and so forth.

Commas with Conditional Sentences

Conditional sentences often use 'if' to introduce a condition. The use of commas depends on the order of the clauses.

When the dependent clause (condition) comes first, a comma is used to separate it from the independent clause:

Example:

If it rains, we will cancel the picnic.

Here, "If it rains" is the dependent clause that sets a condition for "we will cancel the picnic", the independent clause.

When the independent clause comes first, no comma is needed before the dependent clause:

Example:

We will cancel the picnic if it rains.

In this structure, the independent clause "We will cancel the picnic" is followed by the dependent clause "if it rains", so no comma is used.

Using Commas in Complex Sentences

A 'complex sentence' consists of one independent clause and at least one dependent clause. The placement of the comma depends on the order of these clauses.

Dependent clause followed by an independent clause: Use a comma after the dependent clause.

Examples:

Because it was raining, the game was postponed.

Independent clause followed by a dependent clause: Do not use a comma before the dependent clause.

The game was postponed because it was raining.

If she finishes her work, she can go out.

A comma is used because the dependent clause comes first.

She can go out if she finishes her work.

No comma is needed because the independent clause comes first.

In both examples, the clause following 'if' is a dependent clause because it provides a condition and does not stand alone as a complete thought. Thus, when it precedes the main (independent) clause, a comma is used. When it follows the main clause, no comma is necessary.

In summary, the key to using commas correctly with dependent and independent clauses, especially in conditional sentences, is understanding the order of the clauses and whether the clause introduces additional information or sets a condition. Remember, a comma is typically used after a dependent clause when it precedes the independent clause in a sentence. When a dependent clause follows the main clause, a comma is generally not required.

15.2   Practice Makes Perfect

For each of the following sentences, identify whether a comma is needed and correct the sentence accordingly. Use appropriate punctuation to clarify the meaning.

Commas with Conditional Sentences

1. *If you arrive early you can help set up the event.*
   Hint: *The dependent clause comes first.*

2. *We will go to the park if the weather is nice.*
   Hint: *The independent clause comes first.*

3. *If she calls let me know immediately.*
   Hint: *The sentence begins with a dependent clause.*

4. *You will succeed if you work hard.*
   Hint: *The independent clause is followed by a condition.*

5. *If it gets too cold we should head back inside.*
   Hint: *The dependent clause introduces the sentence.*

6. *They will arrive late if there is traffic.*
   Hint: *Check the position of the independent clause.*

7. *If you need assistance please ask the staff.*
   Hint: *The sentence begins with a condition.*

8. *We can start the meeting if everyone is here.*
   Hint: *The condition follows the main clause.*

Commas in Complex Sentences

1. *Although it was raining they decided to go for a walk.*
   Hint: *The dependent clause comes first.*

2. *She stayed home because she was feeling ill.*
   Hint: *The independent clause is followed by a dependent clause.*

3. *Because she was late she missed the bus.*
   Hint: *The sentence begins with a dependent clause.*

4. *The movie was exciting although it was a bit long.*
   Hint: *The independent clause comes first.*

5. *Since it's your birthday you can choose the restaurant.*
   Hint: *The sentence starts with a dependent clause.*

6. *The team won because they practiced hard.*
   Hint: *The independent clause is followed by a reason.*

7. *If you have any questions don't hesitate to ask.*
   Hint: *The sentence begins with a condition.*

8. *They were tired after they completed the marathon.*
   Hint: *The independent clause comes first.*

15.3   PMP Solutions

Commas with Conditional Sentences

1. **Original:** *If you arrive early you can help set up the event.*
   Corrected: *If you arrive early, you can help set up the event.*

2. **Original:** *We will go to the park if the weather is nice.*
   Corrected: *We will go to the park if the weather is nice.* (No correction needed; this is correct as is.)

3. **Original:** *If she calls let me know immediately.*
   Corrected: *If she calls, let me know immediately.*

4. **Original:** *You will succeed if you work hard.*
   Corrected: *You will succeed if you work hard.* (No correction needed; this is correct as is.)

5. **Original:** *If it gets too cold we should head back inside.*
   Corrected: *If it gets too cold, we should head back inside.*

6. **Original:** *They will arrive late if there is traffic.*
   Corrected: *They will arrive late if there is traffic.* (No correction needed; this is correct as is.)

7. **Original:** *If you need assistance please ask the staff.*
   Corrected: *If you need assistance, please ask the staff.*

8. **Original:** *We can start the meeting if everyone is here.*
   Corrected: *We can start the meeting if everyone is here.* (No correction needed; this is correct as is.)

Commas in Complex Sentences

1. **Original:** *Although it was raining they decided to go for a walk.*
   Corrected: *Although it was raining, they decided to go for a walk.*

2. **Original:** *She stayed home because she was feeling ill.*
   Corrected: *She stayed home because she was feeling ill.* (No correction needed; this is correct as is.)

3. **Original:** *Because she was late she missed the bus.*
   Corrected: *Because she was late, she missed the bus.*

4. **Original:** *The movie was exciting although it was a bit long.*
   Corrected: *The movie was exciting, although it was a bit long.*

5. **Original:** *Since it's your birthday you can choose the restaurant.*
   Corrected: *Since it's your birthday, you can choose the restaurant.*

6. **Original:** *The team won because they practiced hard.*
   Corrected: *The team won because they practiced hard.* (No correction needed; this is correct as is.)

7. **Original:** *If you have any questions don't hesitate to ask.*
   Corrected: *If you have any questions, don't hesitate to ask.*

8. **Original:** *They were tired after they completed the marathon.*
   Corrected: *They were tired after they completed the marathon.* (No correction needed; this is correct as is.)

Faster and Fastest

Many word pairs, such as 'maybe' vs. 'may be' and 'further' vs. 'farther', are frequently confused. This chapter breaks down these commonly confused terms, helping readers choose the right word in the appropriate context. §

To compare two or more items, we use the 'comparative form': 'faster'; to describe an item at the extreme upper end of a spectrum, we use the 'superlative form': 'fastest'.

Figure 16.1: Faster and Fastest (Vecteezy Library)

© The Author(s), under exclusive license to Springer Nature Switzerland AG 2024   133
G. Grätzer, *The Little Book of Writing Better*,
https://doi.org/10.1007/978-3-031-76166-9_16

Ensure they are properly used.

Of all the runners in the race, Sarah was faster.

Of all the runners in the race, Sarah was the fastest. 😊

———

Between the two recipes, the chocolate cake is the most popular. 😞

Between the two recipes, the chocolate cake is more popular than the vanilla cake. 😊

———

This smartphone model is the most advanced among all we tested. 😊

———

The red car is faster than the blue one. 😊

16.1   *Maybe vs. May Be*

Figure 16.2: Maybe and May Be (Vecteezy Library)

The distinction between 'maybe' and 'may be' is significant.

'Maybe' is an adverb used to indicate uncertainty or possibility. It typically precedes the subject or serves as a response to a question.

Maybe we can go to the park this weekend. 😊

———

Will it rain tomorrow? Maybe. 😊

'May be' is a verb phrase consisting of the helping verb 'may' and the verb 'be'. It expresses a possibility concerning a state or condition.

The meeting may be rescheduled. 😊

———

There may be a better way to solve this problem. 😊

'Maybe' often appears at the beginning of a sentence or clause, or as a standalone response. 'May be' is part of the predicate and follows the subject.

Consider the sentence structure and what you inrend to express. If you're indicating uncertainty about an entire statement, 'maybe' is appropriate. If you're discussing the potential characteristics or state of a specific subject, 'may be' is the correct choice.

More examples:

Maybe we should try a different restaurant.

———

Maybe next time we should arrive earlier.

———

The discrepancy in the results may be due to a calculation error.

———

There may be a solution we haven't considered yet.

16.2   Further vs. Farther

The distinction between 'further' and 'farther' is subtle. Both can be used for distance or extent, but they are used in slightly different contexts.

Figure 16.3: Further and Farther (Vecteezy Library)

'Farther' refers to physical distance. It is the comparative form of 'far' when discussing tangible, measurable distances.

The next gas station is farther down the road.

———

They moved farther away from the city to find a quieter place to live.

'Further' refers to a metaphorical or figurative distance or to indicate a greater degree or extent in non-physical contexts. It can also imply addition or advancement in time or actions.

More examples:

We need to discuss this issue further.

———

Further investigation is required to determine the cause of the problem.

———

The discussion was continued further into the night.

The distinction between 'farther' and 'further' is becoming increasingly blurred in modern usage, and in many cases, they are used interchangeably.

Note that 'furthermore' is an adverb used to introduce a point that adds to or supports what has already been said. It's similar to 'in addition', 'moreover', or 'besides'.

The project is not feasible at this time. Furthermore, we do not have the necessary resources to support it. 😊

16.3   *Shall vs. Will*

Both 'shall' and 'will' are helping verbs indicating future tense.

The 80% Rule: Always use 'will'.

But do not tell this to General Douglas MacArthur. The title of his famous speech on March 20, 1942:

I Shall Return.

Shall

'Shall' is traditionally used with 'I' and 'we' to express the future tense. It implies formality, determination, or obligation. In legal documents, it is used to state a legal requirement or obligation.

We shall now begin the presentation. 😊

We shall provide a detailed report in the next meeting. 😊

Will

'Will' is used with all subjects (I, you, he, she, it, we, they) to indicate the future tense. It expresses a future action or a willingness or promise to perform a future action.

We will start the project next week. 😊

I will call you when I arrive. 😊

More Illustrations for 'Shall'

We shall explore this topic further in the next chapter. 😊

Shall we proceed with the discussion? 😊

Participants shall submit their feedback by the end of the month. 😊

More Illustrations for 'Will'

This change will likely improve the overall efficiency. 😊

We will review the proposal before making a decision.

———

The team will provide updates on the project's progress during the weekly meeting. 😊

———

I will follow up with you next week. 😊

Contextual Differences

'Shall' is appropriate for formal proposals, methodological discussions, and when outlining requirements or objectives.

The usage of 'will' is more versatile. It is used for casual predictions, descriptions of planned actions, promises, and offers.

Specific Connotations of 'Shall'

Obligation or Requirement:

The new regulations shall apply to all employees. 😊

Strong Intent or Determination:

We shall achieve our goals despite the challenges. 😊

Formality:

Shall we begin the meeting? 😊

Figure 16.4: Forward (Vecteezy Library)

16.4   Foreword vs. Forward

The words 'foreword' and 'forward' sound similar but have entirely different meanings and uses.

Foreword

A 'foreword' is a short introductory section in a book, usually written by someone other than the author.

The foreword by a renowned author sets the tone for the book. 😊

———

In the foreword, the author explains the motivation behind writing the book.

😊

Forward

'Forward' is an adjective, adverb, or verb that denotes direction, progress, or movement towards the front or ahead in time.

> *Looking forward, we will focus on the next phase of the project.* 😊

_____

> *The company is moving forward with its expansion plans.* 😊

_____

> *Please forward the email to the rest of the team.* 😊

16.5   Practice Makes Perfect

Faster and Fastest

Identify whether the comparative or superlative form is needed in the following sentences:

1. Of all the runners in the race, Sarah was _____ (fast). *Hint*: Consider if Sarah is being compared with just one runner or all runners.

2. Between the two recipes, the chocolate cake is _____ (popular) than the vanilla cake. *Hint*: Are you comparing two items or more than two?

3. This route is _____ (short) than the one we took yesterday. *Hint*: Is the comparison between two routes or more?

4. Out of all the candidates, John was the _____ (qualified). *Hint*: Is John being compared to all candidates or just one?

Maybe vs. May Be

Choose the correct form in each sentence:

1. _____ (Maybe/May be) we should consider a different strategy. *Hint*: Is the sentence indicating uncertainty?

2. There _____ (maybe/may be) some truth to what he's saying. *Hint*: Is 'may be' functioning as a verb phrase?

3. The solution _____ (maybe/may be) more complicated than we thought. *Hint*: Is the phrase part of the predicate or indicating uncertainty?

4. _____ (Maybe/May be) it will rain later today. *Hint*: Does this express possibility or a state?

Further vs. Farther

Determine whether 'further' or 'farther' is appropriate:

1. We need to travel _____ (further/farther) to reach the destination. *Hint*: Is the distance physical or metaphorical?

2. The discussion went _____ (further/farther) than expected. *Hint*: Is this about extent in time or physical distance?

3. He pushed the box _____ (further/farther) into the corner. *Hint*: Is this referring to physical movement?

4. The research needs to be taken _____ (further/farther) before conclusions can be drawn. *Hint*: Is the context literal or figurative?

Shall vs. Will

Fill in the blanks with 'shall' or 'will':

1. I _____ call you tomorrow. *Hint*: Consider the formality and intent of each sentence.

2. _____ we go for a walk? *Hint*: Is this a formal question or an informal offer?

3. The committee _____ meet next Thursday. *Hint*: Is this a formal obligation or a future action?

4. I _____ be there on time. *Hint*: Is this a promise or an intention?

Foreword vs. Forward

Choose the correct word:

1. The author included a brief _____ (foreword/forward) in the book. *Hint*: Is this related to a book or direction?

2. Please _____ (foreword/forward) this document to the legal team. *Hint*: Does it involve sending something ahead?

3. The company is moving _____ (foreword/forward) with its expansion plans. *Hint*: Is this about direction or an introduction?

4. The professor wrote the _____ (foreword/forward) for the new edition. *Hint*: Does this refer to a book section or progress?

Not vs. Rather Than

Complete the sentences with 'not' or 'rather than':

1. The decision was based on facts _____ opinions. *Hint*: Is this contrasting two things?

2. I prefer tea _____ coffee. *Hint*: Which word is used to show preference?

3. He chose to walk _____ take the bus. *Hint*: Is this about a choice between two actions?

4. The report highlights data _____ speculation. *Hint*: Is this emphasizing one thing over another?

Cannot vs. Can Not

Select the correct usage:

1. This machine _____ (cannot/can not) operate without electricity. *Hint*: Think about impossibility versus choice.

2. You _____ (cannot/can not) only focus on the results, but also the process. *Hint*: Does it indicate choice or impossibility?

3. They _____ (cannot/can not) agree on the terms. *Hint*: Is it about an inability or a choice?

4. We _____ (cannot/can not) let this opportunity pass. *Hint*: Is this about impossibility or a decision?

Note vs. Notice

Choose the correct word:

1. _____ (Note/Notice) that the deadline is tomorrow. *Hint*: Is this emphasizing an observation or directive?

2. Did you _____ (note/notice) the change in schedule? *Hint*: Is this asking about observation or being informed?

3. Please _____ (note/notice) the instructions before starting. *Hint*: Is this a directive or an observation?

4. I didn't _____ (note/notice) the error in the document. *Hint*: Is this about seeing something or making a note of it?

16.6   PMS Solutions

Faster and Fastest

1. Of all the runners in the race, Sarah was the **fastest**.
2. Between the two recipes, the chocolate cake is **more popular** than the vanilla cake.
3. This route is **shorter** than the one we took yesterday.
4. Out of all the candidates, John was the **most qualified**.

Maybe vs. May Be

1. **Maybe** we should consider a different strategy.
2. There **may be** some truth to what he's saying.
3. The solution **may be** more complicated than we thought.
4. **Maybe** it will rain later today.

Further vs. Farther

1. We need to travel **farther** to reach our destination.
2. The discussion went **further** than expected.
3. He pushed the box **farther** into the corner.
4. The research needs to be taken **further** before conclusions can be drawn.

Shall vs. Will

1. I **will** call you tomorrow.
2. **Shall** we go for a walk?
3. The committee **will** meet next Thursday.
4. I **will** be there on time.

Foreword vs. Forward

1. The author included a brief **foreword** in the book.
2. Please **forward** this document to the legal team.
3. The company is moving **forward** with its expansion plans.
4. The professor wrote the **foreword** to the new edition.

Not vs. Rather Than

1. The decision was based on facts **rather than** opinions.
2. I prefer tea **rather than** coffee.
3. He chose to walk **rather than** take the bus.
4. The report highlights data **rather than** speculation.

Cannot vs. Can Not

1. This machine **cannot** operate without electricity.
2. You **can not** only focus on the results, but also the process.
3. They **cannot** agree on the terms.
4. We **cannot** let this opportunity pass.

Note vs. Notice

1. **Note** that the deadline is tomorrow.
2. Did you **notice** the change in schedule?
3. Please **note** the instructions before starting.
4. I didn't **notice** the error in the document.

17

To Go or Going

This chapter explores the differences between infinitive forms (to go) and gerunds (going), guiding readers on when to use each form. Understanding these differences is essential for constructing sentences that sound natural and grammatically correct. **§**

17.1 The To-Form and the Ing-Form

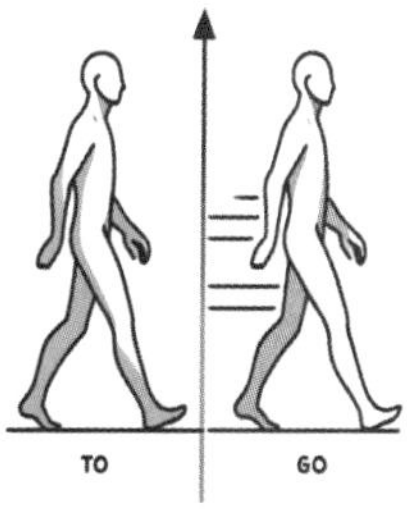

For the verb 'go', the form 'to go' is called the 'to-form' (or 'infinitive').

Everybody remembers Star Trek: "To boldly go where no man has gone before."

Figure 17.1: To go and going (Vecteezy Library)

The 'ing-form', 'going', is the counterpart to the 'to-form' (grammarians call the 'ing-form' a 'gerund').

Examples:

To learn a new language requires dedication and practice. (to-form)

G. Grätzer, *The Little Book of Writing Better*,
https://doi.org/10.1007/978-3-031-76166-9_17

Learning to play the guitar takes time and effort. (ing-form) 😊

—

The goal is to finish the project before the deadline. (to-form) 😊

—

Going to the gym regularly is important for maintaining good health. (ing-form) 😊

Interchanging the 'to-form' with the 'ing-form' can lead to confusion:

I stopped to eat. 😞
vs.
I stopped eating. 😊

17.2   Full and Incomplete Infinitives

Since we will discuss the 'to-form' without the 'to', it is time to use the term 'infinitive'. An 'infinitive' is the basic form of a verb, preceded by the word 'to'. But it can appear in two forms: as 'full infinitive' when 'to' is included, and as 'incomplete infinitive' when 'to' is omitted.

Full Infinitive

The 'full infinitive' is used in various ways, including as a noun, an adjective, or an adverb to explain the reason or objective behind an action.

Typical examples:

To learn is important. 😊

—

I want to finish this book by tomorrow. 😊

—

She seems to understand the concept. 😊

—

To succeed in life, one must work hard. 😊

—

To travel the world is my dream. 😊

—

The recipe is easy to follow. 😊

Incomplete Infinitive

'Incomplete infinitives' often appear after helping verbs (can, could, will, would, shall, should, may, might, must) or certain other verbs (let, make, see, hear, help, and sometimes feel, watch, notice).

Examples:

We can achieve our goals with determination.

I will call you later. 😊

———

This shortcut helps us save time. 😊

———

I saw the car speed away. 😊

17.3 Split Infinitive

A 'split infinitive' occurs when an adverb or other word is inserted between 'to' and the verb in an 'infinitive', as in the Star Trek quote.

Borrowing a rule of Latin grammar, grammarians of English traditionally considered 'split infinitives' incorrect. In Latin, 'infinitives' are single words and thus incapable of being split. However, this view has changed over time. Modern English usage accepts 'split infinitives', especially when they enhance clarity or produce a more natural-sounding sentence.

Examples:

To quickly respond to an email shows good communication skills. 😊

———

To clearly state your intentions is important. 😊

———

To simply explain the process, let's use an example. 😊

———

To honestly answer your question, I don't know. 😊

17.4 Practice Makes Perfect

For each of the following sentences, correct any issues with the use of the 'to-form' or 'ing-form'. Use appropriate punctuation and structure.

The To-form and the Ing-form

1. *He enjoys to read books.*
   Hint: *Consider whether the 'to-form' or the 'ing-form' is more appropriate after 'enjoys'.*

2. *To swim is fun during the summer.*
   Hint: *Determine if the 'to-form' is correctly used or if the 'ing-form' would be better.*

3. *I prefer eating at home rather than to go out.*
   Hint: *Ensure consistency in the forms used in parallel constructions.*

4. *She decided going to the store after work.*
   Hint: *Check if the 'ing-form' is correctly used with 'decided'.*

5. *To exercise daily is good for your health.*
   Hint: *Verify if the 'to-form' is correctly used at the beginning of the sentence.*

6. *They stopped to talk on the phone while walking.*
   Hint: *Determine if the 'to-form' or the 'ing-form' is better in this context.*

7. *My hobby is to collect stamps.*
   Hint: *Consider if the 'ing-form' is more appropriate after 'is'.*

8. *Going to the beach is my favorite summer activity.*
   Hint: *Check if the 'ing-form' is correctly used at the beginning of the sentence.*

Full and Incomplete Infinitives

1. *She wants to quickly finish her homework.*
   Hint: *Consider the position of the adverb 'quickly' in relation to the 'infinitive'.*

2. *We can to start the meeting now.*
   Hint: *Verify if the 'infinitive' is correctly used after 'can'.*

3. *They might to join us for dinner.*
   Hint: *Check the 'infinitive' form after the helping verb 'might'.*

4. *To bake a cake requires patience.*
   Hint: *Confirm if the 'to-form' is correctly used as the subject of the sentence.*

5. *He made me to apologize for the mistake.*
   Hint: *Ensure that the correct 'infinitive' form is used after 'made'.*

6. *We should to leave early tomorrow.*
   Hint: *Verify the use of the 'infinitive' after the modal verb 'should'.*

7. *I can to help you with your homework.*
   Hint: *Check if the 'infinitive' is correctly used after 'can'.*

8. *She needs to finish her project by tomorrow.*
   Hint: *Ensure that the 'to-form' is correctly used after 'needs'.*

Split Infinitives

1. *To thoroughly understand the topic, you need to study.*
   Hint: *Consider if 'thoroughly' is correctly placed within the 'infinitive'.*

2. *To always be on time is important for success.*
   Hint: *Determine if 'always' is properly placed in the sentence.*

3. *He tried to quietly leave the room.*
   Hint: *Check the position of 'quietly' in the 'infinitive'.*

4. *To correctly solve the puzzle, focus on the clues.*
   Hint: *Ensure that 'correctly' is correctly positioned in the sentence.*

5. *To effectively manage your time, create a schedule.*
   Hint: *Consider the position of 'effectively' in the 'infinitive'.*

6. *To quickly answer the question, he raised his hand.*
   Hint: *Check if 'quickly' is correctly placed in the sentence.*

7. *To clearly express your ideas, use simple language.*
   Hint: *Verify the placement of 'clearly' in the 'infinitive'.*

8. *To fully understand the concept, you must practice.*
   Hint: *Consider the placement of 'fully' within the 'infinitive'.*

17.5   PMP Solutions

Here are the solutions to the Practice Makes Perfect exercises.

The To-form and the Ing-form

1. **Original:** *He enjoys to read books.*
   Corrected: *He enjoys reading books.*

2. **Original:** *To swim is fun during the summer.*
   Corrected: *Swimming is fun during the summer.*

3. **Original:** *I prefer eating at home rather than to go out.*
   Corrected: *I prefer eating at home rather than going out.*

4. **Original:** *She decided going to the store after work.*
   Corrected: *She decided to go to the store after work.*

5. **Original:** *To exercise daily is good for your health.*
   Corrected: *Exercising daily is good for your health.*

6. **Original:** *They stopped to talk on the phone while walking.*
   Corrected: *They stopped talking on the phone while walking.*

7. **Original:** *My hobby is to collect stamps.*
   Corrected: *My hobby is collecting stamps.*

8. **Original:** *Going to the beach is my favorite summer activity.*
   Corrected: *Going to the beach is my favorite summer activity.*

Full and Incomplete Infinitives

1. **Original:** *She wants to quickly finish her homework.*
   Corrected: *She wants to finish her homework quickly.*

2. **Original:** *We can to start the meeting now.*
   Corrected: *We can start the meeting now.*

3. **Original:** *They might to join us for dinner.*
   Corrected: *They might join us for dinner.*

4. **Original:** *To bake a cake requires patience.*
   Corrected: *Baking a cake requires patience.*

5. **Original:** *He made me to apologize for the mistake.*
   Corrected: *He made me apologize for the mistake.*

6. **Original:** *We should to leave early tomorrow.*
   Corrected: *We should leave early tomorrow.*

7. **Original:** *I can to help you with your homework.*
   Corrected: *I can help you with your homework.*

8. **Original:** *She needs to finish her project by tomorrow.*
   Corrected: *She needs to finish her project by tomorrow.*

Split Infinitives

1. **Original:** *To thoroughly understand the topic, you need to study.*
   Corrected: *To understand the topic thoroughly, you need to study.*

2. **Original:** *To always be on time is important for success.*
   Corrected: *To be always on time is important for success.*

3. **Original:** *He tried to quietly leave the room.*
   Corrected: *He tried to leave the room quietly.*

4. **Original:** *To correctly solve the puzzle, focus on the clues.*
   Corrected: *To solve the puzzle correctly, focus on the clues.*

5. **Original:** *To effectively manage your time, create a schedule.*
   Corrected: *To manage your time effectively, create a schedule.*

6. **Original:** *To quickly answer the question, he raised his hand.*
   Corrected: *To answer the question quickly, he raised his hand.*

7. **Original:** *To clearly express your ideas, use simple language.*
   Corrected: *To express your ideas clearly, use simple language.*

8. **Original:** *To fully understand the concept, you must practice.*
   Corrected: *To understand the concept fully, you must practice.*

PART IV

And Some More

As, And, Or...
Conjunctions

Conjunctions are vital for linking ideas smoothly. This chapter examines the proper use of 'as', 'and', and 'or', explaining how they can be used effectively to connect clauses and ideas within a sentence. **S**

Figure 18.1: The conjunction 'or' (Vecteezy Library)

© The Author(s), under exclusive license to Springer Nature Switzerland AG 2024   153
G. Grätzer, *The Little Book of Writing Better*,
https://doi.org/10.1007/978-3-031-76166-9_18

18.1   Some Conjunctions

Conjunctions are words that join together other words, phrases, clauses, or sentences, such as 'as', 'and', 'but', 'or', 'yet', 'although'.

You're given a set of instructions in everyday scenarios, and understanding conjunctions will help you follow them correctly.

For example:

Choose books that are both interesting and *informative.*

The conjunction 'and' requires that both conditions be met simultaneously. The books must be both interesting and informative.

However, consider the following instruction:

Choose desserts that are sweet and salty.

This is incorrect because a dessert typically cannot be both sweet and salty at the same time in a conventional sense. The conjunction here connects two mutually exclusive conditions.

Another example:

Select outfits that are comfortable and *suitable for work.*

This statement uses a conjunction appropriately, combining two conditions that can simultaneously apply to several outfits.

18.2   Correct Use

Conjunctions are essential for connecting ideas. Here are a few rules and examples to illustrate proper usage:

The Conjunction 'And'

The conjunction 'and' is used to connect words, phrases, or clauses that have equal importance and are not mutually exclusive.

She bought apples and *oranges.*

In this sentence, 'and' connects two items that are equally important and not mutually exclusive.

The Conjunction 'Or'

The conjunction 'or' is used to offer a choice between two or more options.

Would you like tea or *coffee?*

In this sentence, 'or' presents two choices, only one of which can be selected.

The Conjunction 'But'

The conjunction 'but' is used to connect contrasting ideas.

She is kind but *strict.*

In this sentence, 'but' highlights the contrast between being kind and strict.

The Conjunction 'Yet'

The conjunction 'yet' is used to introduce a contrasting idea that follows logically.

> *He is young,* yet *he is very wise.* 😊
>
> In this sentence, 'yet' shows a contrast between his youth and his wisdom.

18.3 Practice Makes Perfect

For each of the following sentences, identify and correct any issues with conjunction usage. Use appropriate conjunctions to clarify the meaning.

Using 'And' Correctly

1. *She enjoys reading and to paint.*
   Hint: *Ensure that both parts connected by 'and' are parallel in structure.*

2. *He wants to visit Paris and to Rome.*
   Hint: *Consider the consistency of the infinitive form after 'and.'*

3. *The children played games and they watched a movie.*
   Hint: *Determine if the conjunction correctly connects the actions.*

4. *Please bring your ID and fill out this form.*
   Hint: *Check if the structure is parallel and consistent after 'and.'*

5. *She is intelligent and works hard.*
   Hint: *Ensure both clauses connected by 'and' have equal importance.*

6. *They went to the store and to the park.*
   Hint: *Verify parallelism after 'and.'*

7. *The cake is delicious and the frosting is sweet.*
   Hint: *Check if 'and' connects the clauses logically.*

8. *He likes hiking and to swim.*
   Hint: *Consider the structure for parallelism after 'and.'*

Using 'Or' Correctly

1. *Would you like juice milk or something else?*
   Hint: *Consider how many options 'or' is connecting and how to phrase it correctly.*

2. *Choose a day: Monday, Wednesday, or.*
   Hint: *Ensure the conjunction 'or' completes the list of choices.*

3. *Do you prefer to walk or drive?*
   Hint: *Verify that the options are logically connected and complete.*

4. *You can have cake or or pie.*
   Hint: *Check for redundancy or repetition with the conjunction 'or.'*

5. *Do you want tea or coffee or water?*
   Hint: *Ensure the list of options is clear and not confusing.*

6. *Would you prefer to stay home or to go out?*
   Hint: *Consider the balance of the options connected by 'or.'*

7. *She might buy a car or or a bike.*
   Hint: *Verify there's no repetition of 'or.'*

8. *Is it better to study in the morning or or at night?*
   Hint: *Ensure 'or' is correctly used without redundancy.*

Using 'But' Correctly

1. *She is tall but she can play basketball well.*
   Hint: *Ensure that the conjunction 'but' correctly introduces a contrast.*

2. *He wanted to go to the party but, he was tired.*
   Hint: *Consider the placement of the comma in relation to 'but.'*

3. *I would like to join you, but I have a meeting.*
   Hint: *Check if the conjunction 'but' correctly introduces a contrasting idea.*

4. *It was raining but I forgot my umbrella.*
   Hint: *Determine if the conjunction 'but' is used to contrast appropriately.*

5. *He is rich but unhappy.*
   Hint: *Ensure 'but' correctly introduces a contrast.*

6. *She is smart but lazy.*
   Hint: *Verify that 'but' introduces a logical contrast.*

7. *The meal was expensive but delicious.*
   Hint: *Check if 'but' is used to contrast effectively.*

8. *The weather was cold but sunny.*
   Hint: *Ensure that 'but' contrasts the conditions logically.*

Using 'Yet' Correctly

1. *She is very talented, yet her work is not recognized.*
   Hint: *Check if 'yet' is correctly used to show contrast between talent and recognition.*

2. *He studied hard, yet he failed the exam.*
   Hint: *Ensure that 'yet' appropriately connects the contrasting ideas.*

3. *The weather was bad, yet we decided to go hiking.*
   Hint: *Verify that 'yet' introduces a contrast that follows logically.*

4. *I like chocolate, yet I prefer vanilla ice cream.*
   Hint: *Confirm that 'yet' is used to introduce a contrasting preference.*

5. *The project was challenging, yet we completed it on time.*
   Hint: *Ensure 'yet' is used to contrast the challenge with the successful completion.*

6. *He is wealthy, yet he lives modestly.*
   Hint: *Verify the contrast introduced by 'yet.'*

7. *The book was long, yet it was engaging.*
   Hint: *Ensure 'yet' connects the contrast logically.*

8. *She was tired, yet she continued working.*
   Hint: *Confirm 'yet' is used correctly to show the contrast in actions.*

18.4   PMP Solutions

Using 'And' Correctly

1. **Original:** *She enjoys reading and to paint.*
   Corrected: *She enjoys reading and painting.*

2. **Original:** *He wants to visit Paris and to Rome.*
   Corrected: *He wants to visit Paris and Rome.*

3. **Original:** *The children played games and they watched a movie.*
   Corrected: *The children played games and watched a movie.*

4. **Original:** *Please bring your ID and fill out this form.*
   Corrected: *Please bring your ID and fill out this form.*

5. **Original:** *She is intelligent and works hard.*
   Corrected: *She is intelligent and hardworking.*

6. **Original:** *They went to the store and to the park.*
   Corrected: *They went to the store and the park.*

7. **Original:** *The cake is delicious and the frosting is sweet.*
   Corrected: *The cake and frosting are delicious and sweet.*

8. **Original:** *He likes hiking and to swim.*
   Corrected: *He likes hiking and swimming.*

Using 'Or' Correctly

1. **Original:** *Would you like juice milk or something else?*
   Corrected: *Would you like juice or milk or something else?*

2. **Original:** *Choose a day: Monday, Wednesday, or.*
   Corrected: *Choose a day: Monday, Wednesday, or Friday.*

3. **Original:** *Do you prefer to walk or drive?*
   Corrected: *Do you prefer to walk or drive?*

4. **Original:** *You can have cake or or pie.*
   Corrected: *You can have cake or pie.*

5. **Original:** *Do you want tea or coffee or water?*
   Corrected: *Do you want tea, coffee, or water?*

6. **Original:** *Would you prefer to stay home or to go out?*
   Corrected: *Would you prefer to stay home or go out?*

7. **Original:** *She might buy a car or or a bike.*
   Corrected: *She might buy a car or a bike.*

8. **Original:** *Is it better to study in the morning or or at night?*
   Corrected: *Is it better to study in the morning or at night?*

Using 'But' Correctly

1. **Original:** *She is tall but she can play basketball well.*
   Corrected: *She is tall, but she can play basketball well.*

2. **Original:** *He wanted to go to the party but, he was tired.*
   Corrected: *He wanted to go to the party, but he was tired.*

3. **Original:** *I would like to join you, but I have a meeting.*
   Corrected: *I would like to join you, but I have a meeting.*

4. **Original:** *It was raining but I forgot my umbrella.*
   Corrected: *It was raining, but I forgot my umbrella.*

5. **Original:** *He is rich but unhappy.*
   Corrected: *He is rich, but unhappy.*

6. **Original:** *She is smart but lazy.*
   Corrected: *She is smart, but lazy.*

7. **Original:** *The meal was expensive but delicious.*
   Corrected: *The meal was expensive, but delicious.*

8. **Original:** *The weather was cold but sunny.*
   Corrected: *The weather was cold, but sunny.*

Using 'Yet' Correctly

1. **Original:** *She is very talented, yet her work is not recognized.*
   Corrected: *She is very talented, yet her work is not recognized.*

2. **Original:** *He studied hard, yet he failed the exam.*
   Corrected: *He studied hard, yet he failed the exam.*

3. **Original:** *The weather was bad, yet we decided to go hiking.*
   Corrected: *The weather was bad, yet we decided to go hiking.*

4. **Original:** *I like chocolate, yet I prefer vanilla ice cream.*
   Corrected: *I like chocolate, yet I prefer vanilla ice cream.*

5. **Original:** *The project was challenging, yet we completed it on time.*
   Corrected: *The project was challenging, yet we completed it on time.*

6. **Original:** *He is wealthy, yet he lives modestly.*
   Corrected: *He is wealthy, yet he lives modestly.*

7. **Original:** *The book was long, yet it was engaging.*
   Corrected: *The book was long, yet it was engaging.*

8. **Original:** *She was tired, yet she continued working.*
   Corrected: *She was tired, yet she continued working.*

19

'Either', 'Or', 'Both'... More Conjunctions

Building on the previous chapter, this section delves into more complex conjunctions such as 'either', 'or', and 'both'. Readers will learn how to use these conjunctions to add precision and subtlety to their writing.

19.1 More Conjunctions

Conjunctions like 'either', 'or', and 'both' are small but powerful words that help in linking ideas, options, and conditions in everyday language. Understanding how to use them correctly can make your writing clearer and more precise.

Either

'Either' signifies one out of two mutually exclusive options.

Examples:

You can have either tea or coffee.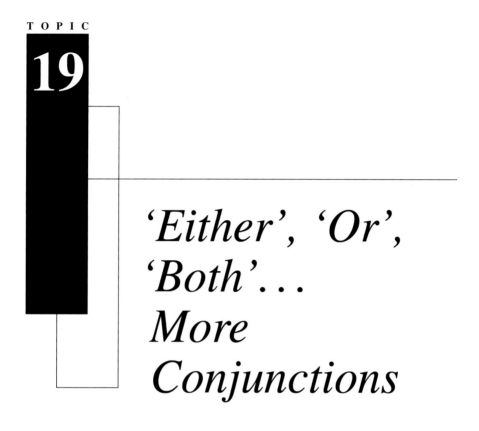

In this sentence, 'either' presents two distinct choices, and only one can be selected.

G. Grätzer, *The Little Book of Writing Better*,
https://doi.org/10.1007/978-3-031-76166-9_19

She will either go to the party or stay home. 😊

Here, 'either' introduces two mutually exclusive possibilities: attending the party or staying home.

Or

'Or' links alternatives and does not always signify an exclusive relationship.

Exclusive use (implied by context):

Would you prefer to visit the museum or the park? 😊

In this case, 'or' offers two distinct choices, but not both.

Inclusive use:

You can study history or literature, or both. 😊

Here, 'or' allows for one option, the other, or both to be chosen.

Both

'Both' is used to indicate that two conditions or statements are applicable simultaneously.

Examples:

She is both intelligent and hardworking. 😊

In this sentence, 'both' confirms that two qualities apply to the subject.

You need to bring both your ID and passport. 😊

Here, 'both' emphasizes that two items are required.

Either... Or

An 'either... or' statement presents two mutually exclusive options, implying that if one is true, the other must be false.

Either the lights are on, or the room is dark. 😊

This sentence presents two opposite scenarios, only one of which can be true at any given time.

19.2   Practice Makes Perfect

For each of the following sentences, identify and correct any issues with the use of 'either', 'or', and 'both'. Use appropriate rephrasing to clarify the meaning.

Using 'Either' Correctly

1. *You can either choose to walk or by car.*
   Hint: *Ensure that 'either' properly introduces two clear choices.*

2. *Either John or Sally are going to lead the meeting.*
   Hint: *Consider the subject-verb agreement with 'either... or'.*

3. *She can either read a book or watching TV.*
   Hint: *Ensure parallel structure after 'either'.*

4. *You can either go to the beach or to the mountains.*
   Hint: *Consider if the structure is consistent and clear.*

5. *The dessert can either be cake or ice cream.*
   Hint: *Ensure that the options presented are parallel in structure.*

6. *You can either attend the morning session or the afternoon.*
   Hint: *Check for consistency in the options provided after 'either'.*

7. *She will either call you or sending a message.*
   Hint: *Make sure that the actions after 'either' are in parallel form.*

8. *You can either come early or staying late.*
   Hint: *Ensure that both choices are in parallel form after 'either'.*

Using 'Or' Correctly

1. *Would you like coffee, tea, or?*
   Hint: *Ensure that 'or' completes the list of options.*

2. *You can choose pizza, salad, or both.*
   Hint: *Verify if 'or' is used correctly to indicate an inclusive choice.*

3. *Do you want to watch a movie or go for a walk?*
   Hint: *Check if the options connected by 'or' are parallel and logical.*

4. *We can go hiking, or we could stay home.*
   Hint: *Ensure the options after 'or' are presented consistently.*

5. *Will you have cake or have pie?*
   Hint: *Consider if the repetition is necessary or if it can be simplified.*

6. *You should either write an essay or or take a test.*
   Hint: *Avoid redundancy when using 'or'.*

7. *Would you rather swim in the pool or the lake?*
   Hint: *Ensure the options are clearly connected by 'or'.*

8. *Would you like to eat out or to cook at home?*
   Hint: *Check for parallelism in the options provided after 'or'.*

Using 'Both' Correctly

1. *She is both kind and she is generous.*
   Hint: *Ensure that 'both' introduces parallel qualities or actions.*

2. *You need to bring both your keys, and also your wallet.*
   Hint: *Consider if 'both' is used correctly without redundancy.*

3. *The course covers both theory as well as practical skills.*
   Hint: *Ensure that 'both' is not used redundantly with other conjunctions.*

4. *I want to visit both Paris, and Rome.*
   Hint: *Verify the proper use of 'both' with multiple items.*

5. *He is both a good listener and he also gives great advice.*
   Hint: *Check for unnecessary repetition after 'both'.*

6. *She enjoys both reading books and to write stories.*
   Hint: *Ensure parallelism in the activities listed after 'both'.*

7. *The project requires both creativity and to work hard.*
   Hint: *Consider if the actions are parallel and consistent after 'both'.*

8. *You can either take both classes or only one.*
   Hint: *Ensure that 'both' is used logically in context with 'either'.*

Using 'Either... Or' Correctly

1. *You can either stay here or leaving with us.*
   Hint: *Ensure that both choices presented are parallel in structure.*

2. *Either the team wins, or it loses.*
   Hint: *Ensure the structure is consistent and clear.*

3. *You can either take a nap or going for a walk.*
   Hint: *Verify that the actions after 'either' are parallel in form.*

4. *Either you agree with the terms, or you not sign the contract.*
   Hint: *Check the agreement and parallelism of the options presented.*

5. *He will either come with us or staying home.*
   Hint: *Ensure parallelism in the options presented with 'either... or'.*

6. *Either you can study for the exam or not prepare at all.*
   Hint: *Make sure the options are logical and clearly contrasted.*

7. *Either we leave now, or we missing the show.*
   Hint: *Ensure that both clauses after 'either... or' are parallel in structure.*

8. *You can either watch TV or playing video games.*
   Hint: *Check that both activities are presented in a parallel form.*

19.3 PMP Solutions

Here are the solutions to the Practice Makes Perfect exercises.

Using 'Either' Correctly

1. **Original:** *You can either choose to walk or by car.*
   Corrected: *You can either walk or go by car.*

2. **Original:** *Either John or Sally are going to lead the meeting.*
   Corrected: *Either John or Sally is going to lead the meeting.*

3. **Original:** *She can either read a book or watching TV.*
   Corrected: *She can either read a book or watch TV.*

4. **Original:** *You can either go to the beach or to the mountains.*
   Corrected: *You can either go to the beach or go to the mountains.*

5. **Original:** *The dessert can either be cake or ice cream.*
   Corrected: *The dessert can be either cake or ice cream.*

6. **Original:** *You can either attend the morning session or the afternoon.*
   Corrected: *You can attend either the morning session or the afternoon session.*

7. **Original:** *She will either call you or sending a message.*
   Corrected: *She will either call you or send a message.*

8. **Original:** *You can either come early or staying late.*
   Corrected: *You can either come early or stay late.*

Using 'Or' Correctly

1. **Original:** *Would you like coffee, tea, or?*
   Corrected: *Would you like coffee, tea, or something else?*

2. **Original:** *You can choose pizza, salad, or both.*
   Corrected: *You can choose pizza, salad, or you can have both.*

3. **Original:** *Do you want to watch a movie or go for a walk?*
   Corrected: *Do you want to watch a movie or take a walk?*

4. **Original:** *We can go hiking, or we could stay home.*
   Corrected: *We can go hiking, or we can stay home.*

5. **Original:** *Will you have cake or have pie?*
   Corrected: *Will you have cake or pie?*

6. **Original:** *You should either write an essay or or take a test.*
   Corrected: *You should either write an essay or take a test.*

7. **Original:** *Would you rather swim in the pool or the lake?*
   Corrected: *Would you rather swim in the pool or in the lake?*

8. **Original:** *Would you like to eat out or to cook at home?*
   Corrected: *Would you like to eat out or cook at home?*

Using 'Both' Correctly

1. **Original:** *She is both kind and she is generous.*
   Corrected: *She is both kind and generous.*

2. **Original:** *You need to bring both your keys, and also your wallet.*
   Corrected: *You need to bring both your keys and your wallet.*

3. **Original:** *The course covers both theory as well as practical skills.*
   Corrected: *The course covers both theory and practical skills.*

4. **Original:** *I want to visit both Paris, and Rome.*
   Corrected: *I want to visit both Paris and Rome.*

5. **Original:** *He is both a good listener and he also gives great advice.*
   Corrected: *He is both a good listener and gives great advice.*

6. **Original:** *She enjoys both reading books and to write stories.*
   Corrected: *She enjoys both reading books and writing stories.*

7. **Original:** *The project requires both creativity and to work hard.*
   Corrected: *The project requires both creativity and hard work.*

8. **Original:** *You can either take both classes or only one.*
   Corrected: *You can either take both classes or just one.*

Using 'Either... Or' Correctly

1. **Original:** *You can either stay here or leaving with us.*
   Corrected: *You can either stay here or leave with us.*

2. **Original:** *Either the team wins, or it loses.*
   Corrected: *Either the team wins, or it loses.* (No correction needed; this is correct as is.)

3. **Original:** *You can either take a nap or going for a walk.*
   Corrected: *You can either take a nap or go for a walk.*

4. **Original:** *Either you agree with the terms, or you not sign the contract.*
   Corrected: *Either you agree with the terms, or you don't sign the contract.*

5. **Original:** *He will either come with us or staying home.*
   Corrected: *He will either come with us or stay home.*

6. **Original:** *Either you can study for the exam or not prepare at all.*
   Corrected: *Either you can study for the exam or not prepare at all.* (No correction needed; this is correct as is.)

7. **Original:** *Either we leave now, or we missing the show.*
   Corrected: *Either we leave now, or we miss the show.*

8. **Original:** *You can either watch TV or playing video games.*
   Corrected: *You can either watch TV or play video games.*

Less and Fewer, Both and Two

The distinction between 'less' and 'fewer' is important for ensuring grammatical accuracy, as is the difference between 'both' and 'two'. This chapter explains how to use these terms correctly, improving

20.1 Less and Fewer

The distinction between 'less' and 'fewer' is straightforward: 'fewer' refers to items that can be counted (discrete quantities), while 'less' is used for measurable (continuous, uncountable) quantities. Let's explore examples to clarify their proper use and illustrate common misuse.

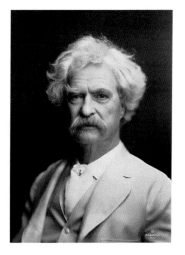

Figure 20.1: Mark Twain
(Vecteezy Library)

© The Author(s), under exclusive license to Springer Nature Switzerland AG 2024   169
G. Grätzer, *The Little Book of Writing Better*,
https://doi.org/10.1007/978-3-031-76166-9_20

Examples of Correct Usage

There are fewer students in class today than yesterday. 😊
  Students can be counted.
  I solved fewer problems today than I did last week. 😊
  Problems are discrete items.
  I spent less time on homework today than I did last week. 😊
  Time is a continuous quantity.

Examples of Incorrect Usage

This recipe requires fewer sugar than the other one. 😞
  Sugar, when not specified in units like cups or tablespoons, should be treated as
a continuous quantity.

  There are less cars in the parking lot today. 😞
  There are fewer cars in the parking lot today. 😊

  There are less people in line today than yesterday. 😞
  There are fewer people in line today than yesterday. 😊

20.2   Both and Two

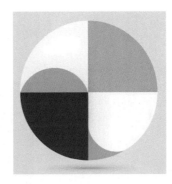

Figure 20.2: Both and Two (Vecteezy Library)

The definition is straightforward: 'both' refers to a shared property of two items,
while 'two' counts the items.
  Examples:
  Both my brother and sister are tall. 😊
  The two siblings share the property of being tall.
  To complete the puzzle, both pieces must fit together perfectly. 😊
  It correctly specifies a condition involving two elements.
  The two children played together all afternoon. 😊
  This specifies the number of children.

Both of the two solutions to the problem are correct. 😩
The phrase 'both of the two' is redundant because 'both' already implies 'two'.
Two of the participants were selected for the prize. 😊
This specifies a quantity related to the elements described.
Both options are available to you. 😊
It indicates that two options are simultaneously available.

20.3   Practice Makes Perfect

For each of the following sentences, choose the correct word or phrase to complete
the sentence. Use the hints if you need help.

1. There are ____ books on the shelf than yesterday.
   Hint: *Are books countable or measurable?*

2. She has ____ sugar in her coffee than before.
   Hint: *Is sugar in this context countable or measurable?*

3. Both options ____ available for the job position.
   Hint: *Are we talking about one or two options?*

4. The ____ dogs are playing in the yard.
   Hint: *Are you focusing on the quantity or shared characteristics of the dogs?*

5. He bought ____ apples than I did.
   Hint: *Can apples be counted?*

6. The recipe requires ____ flour than I expected.
   Hint: *Is flour in this context countable or measurable?*

7. Both ____ of the puzzle pieces are missing.
   Hint: *Is the phrase 'both of the two' redundant?*

8. The two children ____ playing quietly.
   Hint: *Are you focusing on the number of children or their shared activity?*

20.4   PMP Solutions

Here are the solutions to the Practice Makes Perfect exercises:

1. **Correct Answer:** *fewer*
   There are fewer books on the shelf than yesterday.

2. **Correct Answer:** *less*
   She has less sugar in her coffee than before.

3. **Correct Answer:** *are*
   Both options are available for the job position.

4. **Correct Answer:** *two*
   The two dogs are playing in the yard.

5. **Correct Answer:** *fewer*
   He bought fewer apples than I did.

6. **Correct Answer:** *less*
   The recipe requires less flour than I expected.

7. **Correct Answer:** *pieces*
   Both pieces of the puzzle are missing.

8. **Correct Answer:** *are*
   The two children are playing quietly.

Modifiers

Modifiers can be adjectives, which modify nouns, or adverbs, which modify verbs, adjectives, or other adverbs. Modifiers add detail and color to writing, but they can also create confusion if misplaced. This topic explains how to use modifiers effectively, avoiding common mistakes like dangling and misplaced modifiers. §

21.1 Guidelines for Using Modifiers

Accuracy and Necessity Use only necessary modifiers to convey the correct meaning. Choose precise modifiers, as subtle differences can change the entire meaning of a sentence. For instance, the difference between 'old' and 'very old' can be significant depending on the context.

Placement Place modifiers close to the words they modify, avoiding ambiguity. Avoid dangling modifiers that do not clearly refer to any specific word in the sentence.

Consistency Maintain consistent terminology throughout a document. Switching between different terms or modifiers for the same concept can confuse the reader.

© The Author(s), under exclusive license to Springer Nature Switzerland AG 2024   173
G. Grätzer, *The Little Book of Writing Better*,
https://doi.org/10.1007/978-3-031-76166-9_21

Conciseness Opt for the fewest words that can clearly convey the intended idea while maintaining accuracy. Redundant modifiers can often be eliminated without losing meaning.

21.2   Examples of Modifier Use

Use of Adjectives *The dress is very unique in its design.*
> *The dress is unique in its design.*
> 'Unique' is an absolute quality, so adding 'very' is redundant.

Adjective Misplacement *We bought an expensive new car.*
> *We bought a new expensive car.*
> The placement of 'expensive' and 'new' changes the focus of the description.

Adverbial Clarity *She almost nearly missed the train.*
> *She nearly missed the train.*
> 'Almost nearly' is redundant; 'nearly' alone suffices.

Consistency in Modifiers *He was both happy and very excited.*
> *He was both happy and excited.*
> Maintaining a consistent level of emphasis avoids unnecessary complications.

Redundant Modifiers *The absolutely complete list is available.*
> *The complete list is available.*
> 'Absolutely' is unnecessary as 'complete' already conveys the meaning fully.

Precision in Context *The dog runs fast.*
> *The dog runs at a remarkable speed.*
> Using a more specific description can give a clearer picture of the action.

Avoiding Ambiguity *The man saw the girl with binoculars.*
> *With binoculars, the man saw the girl.*
> Placing 'with binoculars' at the beginning clarifies who is using them.

Dangling Modifiers *Walking through the park, the flowers were beautiful.*
> *Walking through the park, I noticed the beautiful flowers.*
> The corrected sentence clarifies who is walking and noticing the flowers.

Adverb Placement *She quickly ate the cake.*
> *She ate the cake quickly.*
> The adverb 'quickly' placed after the verb 'ate' can sometimes improve the sentence's flow.

21.3   *Practice Makes Perfect*

Exercises

1. Identify the redundant modifier and revise the sentence: *The extremely perfect solution worked.*
   Hint: *Consider whether 'extremely' adds necessary meaning to the adjective 'perfect.'*

2. Correct the misplaced modifier: *She served a cake to the children that was freshly baked.*
   Hint: *Rearrange the sentence to clarify what 'freshly baked' refers to.*

3. Remove the unnecessary modifier: *He completely finished the task.*
   Hint: *Think about whether 'completely' adds any additional meaning to 'finished.'*

4. Rewrite the sentence to avoid ambiguity: *Flying over the city, the buildings looked tiny.*
   Hint: *Clarify who or what is flying over the city.*

5. Adjust the sentence for adverb placement: *She gently put the baby down.*
   Hint: *Consider whether placing 'gently' after the verb improves the flow.*

6. Eliminate redundant modifiers: *The slightly small room was cozy.*
   Hint: *Decide whether both 'slightly' and 'small' are needed.*

7. Correct the modifier for consistency: *He is a talented and very skilled musician.*
   Hint: *Ensure the modifiers 'talented' and 'skilled' are consistent in emphasis.*

8. Revise the sentence to avoid a dangling modifier: *Hiking the trail, the birds were singing beautifully.*
   Hint: *Clarify who is hiking the trail.*

21.4   *PMP Solutions*

Solutions

1. *The perfect solution worked.*
   Reason: 'Extremely' is redundant as 'perfect' already implies the highest degree.

2. *She served the freshly baked cake to the children.*
   Reason: Moving 'freshly baked' before 'cake' clarifies what was baked.

3. *He finished the task.*
   Reason: 'Completely' is unnecessary because 'finished' already means something is done entirely.

4. *As they flew over the city, the buildings looked tiny.*
   Reason: This revision makes it clear who is flying over the city.

5. *She put the baby down gently.*
   Reason: Placing 'gently' after the verb improves the natural flow of the sentence.

6. *The small room was cozy.*
   Reason: 'Slightly' is redundant when 'small' already conveys the necessary meaning.

7. *He is a talented and skilled musician.*
   Reason: The sentence is more balanced without the added 'very,' maintaining consistent emphasis.

8. *While hiking the trail, I noticed the birds singing beautifully.*
   Reason: The revision clarifies that the subject (I) was hiking the trail.

Correction to: The Little Book of Writing Better

Correction to:
G. Grätzer, *The Little Book of Writing Better,*
https://doi.org/10.1007/978-3-031-76166-9

The original version of the book was inadvertently published with the incorrect copyright year 2025 which has now been corrected to 2024. The book has been updated with the changes.

The updated version of this book can be found at
https://doi.org/10.1007/978-3-031-76166-9

A

Grammatical Terms

In this section, we introduce some basic grammatical terms that are used throughout this book. Each term is explained with examples to help you understand how it applies to everyday language.

Noun A noun is a word that names a person, place, thing, or idea.

Figure A.1: Parts of speech (Vecteezy Library)

© The Editor(s) (if applicable) and The Author(s), under exclusive license
to Springer Nature Switzerland AG 2024
G. Grätzer, *The Little Book of Writing Better*,
https://doi.org/10.1007/978-3-031-76166-9

Examples:

- **Person:** The *teacher* gave us homework.

- **Place:** The *library* is quiet.

- **Thing:** I need a new *book*.

- **Idea:** *Freedom* is important.

Pronoun A pronoun is used in place of a noun to avoid repetition.

Examples:

- *It* is raining outside.

- *They* are going to the park.

Verb A verb shows action, occurrence, or state of being.

Examples:

- **Run:** She *runs* every morning.

- **Is:** The cake *is* delicious.

Adjective An adjective describes or modifies a noun.

Examples:

- **Blue:** She wore a *blue* dress.

- **Happy:** The *happy* child smiled.

Adverb An adverb modifies a verb, an adjective, or another adverb. It often describes how, when, where, or to what extent something happens.

Examples:

- **Quickly:** She finished her work *quickly*.

- **Very:** The movie was *very* interesting.

Preposition A preposition shows the relationship between a noun (or pronoun) and other words in a sentence, often indicating position, time, or direction.

Examples:

- **On:** The book is *on* the table.

- **Under:** The keys are *under* the mat.

Conjunction A conjunction connects words, phrases, clauses, or sentences (e.g., and, but, or).

Examples:

- **And:** We bought apples *and* oranges.

- **Or:** You can choose tea *or* coffee.

Interjection An interjection is an exclamation or short utterance that expresses emotion but has no grammatical connection to other words.

Examples:

- **Oops!** I dropped the glass.

- **Aha!** I found the solution.

Subject The subject is the person, place, thing, or idea that is doing or being something in a sentence.

Examples:

- **The dog** barked loudly.

- **This book** is interesting.

Predicate The predicate tells something about the subject, usually containing a verb and providing information about the action or state of being of the subject.

Examples:

- **is running:** The athlete *is running*.

- **will win:** She *will win* the race.

Clause A clause is a group of words containing a subject and a predicate. It can be independent (main clause) or dependent (subordinate clause).

Examples:

- **Main clause:** She sings.

- **Subordinate clause:** If it rains.

Phrase A phrase is a group of words that acts as a single unit in a sentence but does not have both a subject and a verb.

Examples:

- **Under the table:** The cat is *under the table*.

- **With a smile:** He greeted me *with a smile*.

Tense Tense shows the time of the action or state of being indicated by the verb (past, present, future).

Examples:

- **Past:** She *walked* to the store.

- **Present:** He *is reading* a book.

- **Future:** They *will travel* tomorrow.

Article An article is a word used to modify a noun, which is grammatically necessary for noun phrase structure (definite article: the; indefinite articles: a, an).

Examples:

- **The:** *The* cat is on the roof.

- **A:** She saw *a* bird.

Syntax Syntax is the arrangement of words and phrases to create well-formed sentences.

Examples:

- **Syntax in a question:** Where *is* the book?

- **Syntax in a command:** *Close* the door.

Punctuation Punctuation includes symbols that help to structure and organize writing.

Examples:

- **Period (.):** Marks the end of a sentence.

- **Comma (,):** Indicates a pause between parts of a sentence or separates items in a list.

- **Question Mark (?):** Ends a sentence that asks a question.

- **Exclamation Mark (!):** Ends a sentence that expresses strong feelings or commands.

- **Colon (:):** Introduces a list, a quote, or an explanation.

- **Semicolon (;):** Links independent clauses in a sentence or separates items in a list that already includes commas.

- **Apostrophe ('):** Indicates possession or the omission of letters.

- **Quotation Marks (" "):** Enclose direct speech, quotations, or titles.

- **Hyphen (-):** Joins words or parts of words (e.g., twenty-three, well-known).

- **Dash:** The Em-Dash (—) adds emphasis or an interruption.
  The En-Dash (–) indicates ranges or connections.

- **Parentheses (()):** Encloses additional information or clarifications.

- **Brackets [ ]:** Used for technical explanations or to clarify meaning.

- **Ellipsis (...):** Indicates the omission of words or a trailing off of thought.

Sentence types Sentences can be classified based on their structure (simple, compound, complex, compound-complex) and purpose (declarative, interrogative, imperative, exclamatory).

Examples:

- **Declarative:** The sun rises in the east.

- **Imperative:** Please close the door.

- **Interrogative:** What time is it?

- **Exclamatory:** Wow, that's amazing!

Your Grammar Tutor

B.1 Introduction

Working on this book, I had an indispensable assistant: ChatGPT Plus, the subscription service of ChatGPT, introduced in the next section. Often, I turned to it for help with English grammar.

In my discussions and email exchanges with experts, skepticism was a common response: "You know my opinion of ChatGPT and other large language models; they can be misleading, and under certain circumstances, produce entirely captivating yet nonsensical and fabricated content."

This response puzzled me. Each time I consulted ChatGPT, it provided clear and unambiguous answers. To help you gain the same benefits, I decided to write this appendix.

ChatGPT is an LLM (Large Language Model), an artificial intelligence model trained to understand and generate human language. An LLM is 'large' if it is trained on extensive text data, including books, articles, websites, and other digital texts, to grasp language patterns, vocabulary, and grammar.

An LLM can perform various language-related tasks, such as answering questions, completing sentences, and summarizing texts. The OpenAI GPT series (Generative Pre-trained Transformer) are notable examples of LLMs. I have experience only

© The Editor(s) (if applicable) and The Author(s), under exclusive license
to Springer Nature Switzerland AG 2024
G. Grätzer, *The Little Book of Writing Better*,
https://doi.org/10.1007/978-3-031-76166-9

with ChatGPT Plus. Of course, other LLMs would also provide similar assistance.

These large language models have garnered considerable attention for their ability to produce coherent and contextually relevant text, proving invaluable in many different domains ranging from creative writing to technical support and coding.

To start using ChatGPT, visit the website

```
openai.com
```

and start asking questions.

B.2   How ChatGPT Can Help You

ChatGPT is equipped with advanced natural language processing capabilities, allowing it to understand your questions and provide detailed explanations in real-time. Here's how ChatGPT can assist you:

- **Grammar Corrections:** Whether you're unsure about subject-verb agreement, punctuation, or the use of tenses, ChatGPT can review your sentences and suggest corrections.

- **Explanations:** ChatGPT offers clear, concise explanations of grammar rules, helping you understand why certain corrections are necessary.

- **Follow-Up Questions:** Learning is an ongoing process, and ChatGPT encourages you to ask follow-up questions to clarify doubts or explore related topics further.

Here is a simple example. I was not sure how to capitalize the title of Section 17.1: "The To-form and the Ing-form" or "The To-Form and the Ing-Form".

So I asked: *How do you capitalize: "The To-form and the Ing-form" or "The To-Form and the Ing-Form"?*

And ChatGPT responded: *Both phrases, "The To-form and the Ing-form" and "The To-Form and the Ing-Form" are correct, but they follow different capitalization rules:*

The To-form and the Ing-form: This uses sentence-style capitalization, where only the first word and proper nouns or adjectives are capitalized.

The To-Form and the Ing-Form: This uses title-style capitalization, where all major words are capitalized.

Choose based on the style guide you are following or the context in which the title is used. For formal titles or headings, the second option, "The To-Form and the Ing-Form" is typically preferred.

I accepted the advice.

B.3   Follow-Up Questions

Grammar learning is not a one-time event; it's an ongoing process that thrives on curiosity and deeper inquiry. Often, after correcting a sentence or learning a new rule, you may find yourself with additional questions. These follow-up questions are essential for truly mastering grammar, as they help reinforce concepts and ensure that you can apply what you've learned in various contexts.

1. *Correct the following sentence: She don't like to play soccer.*
   Correction: *She doesn't like to play soccer.*
   Follow-Up Question: *Why is 'doesn't' used instead of 'don't'?*
   Answer: *In English, the subject-verb agreement rule requires that the verb form matches the subject. 'She' is a third-person singular pronoun, so the correct auxiliary verb is 'does,' not 'do.' Therefore, 'doesn't' (a contraction of 'does not') is the correct form.*

2. *Choose the correct form: (Who's / Whose) book is this?*
   Correction: *Whose book is this?*
   Follow-Up Question: What is the difference between 'who's' and 'whose'?
   Answer: *'Who's' is a contraction of 'who is' or 'who has,' while 'whose' is a possessive pronoun that indicates ownership. In the sentence 'Whose book is this?', you are asking about the owner of the book, so 'whose' is the correct word.*

3. *Rewrite the sentence to correct the misplaced modifier: Running to catch the bus, the backpack slipped off John's shoulder.*
   Correction: *Running to catch the bus, John's backpack slipped off his shoulder.*
   Follow-Up Question: *Why was it necessary to move 'John' closer to the modifier 'running to catch the bus'?*
   Answer: *Modifiers should be placed next to the word they are meant to modify to avoid confusion. In the original sentence, 'Running to catch the bus' was incorrectly placed next to 'the backpack,' making it seem as though the backpack was running. The correction places 'John' next to the modifier, clarifying that he is the one running.*

4. *Correct the following sentence for parallel structure: She enjoys reading, to write, and going for walks.*
   Correction: *She enjoys reading, writing, and going for walks.*
   Follow-Up Question: *What is parallel structure, and why is it important in this sentence?*
   Answer: *Parallel structure involves using the same grammatical form within a list or series. In this case, 'reading', 'writing', and 'going for walks' should all be in the same form (gerunds) to maintain a balanced and clear sentence structure. This helps improve readability and flow.*

5. *Identify the error in subject-verb agreement: Neither the manager nor the employees was satisfied with the decision.*
   Correction: *Neither the manager nor the employees were satisfied with the decision.*
   Follow-Up Question: *Why was 'were' replaced by 'was' in this sentence?*

Answer: In sentences with 'neither...nor', the verb should agree with the noun closest to it. In this case, 'employees' is plural, so the correct verb is 'were', not 'was.'

6. *Rewrite the sentence to avoid ambiguity: She told her friend that she won the lottery.*

   Correction: *She told her friend, 'I won the lottery.'*

   Follow-Up Question: *How does this correction remove the ambiguity?*

   Answer: *The original sentence could be interpreted in two ways—either 'she' won the lottery, or her friend won the lottery. The correction clarifies that 'she' is the one who won by directly quoting what was said.*

7. *Correct the following sentence for tense consistency: He was walking to the store when he sees an old friend.*

   Correction: *He was walking to the store when he saw an old friend.*

   Follow-Up Question: *Why is it important for tenses to be consistent in a sentence?*

   Answer: *Tense consistency is important because it ensures that the timing of events is clear and logical. In this case, both actions ('was walking' and 'saw') happened in the past, so the tenses should match.*

8. *Identify and correct the dangling participle: After finishing the assignment, the TV was turned on.*

   Correction: *After finishing the assignment, she turned on the TV.*

   Follow-Up Question: *What is a dangling participle, and how does this correction resolve the issue?*

   Answer: *A dangling participle is a participle phrase that is not clearly and logically related to the word it is intended to modify. The original sentence implied that 'the TV' finished the assignment. The correction clarifies that 'she' finished the assignment and then turned on the TV.*

B.4   The Jewel in the Crown

I have two favourite prompts for editing, I call them "The Jewel in the Crown" (a novel by Paul Scott, William Heinemann Ltd, 1966).

The First Jewel: Evaluate

I want to edit two sentences. I use the prompt 'evaluate'.

   evaluate: Her and me went to the store, but we didn't buy nothing. The movie was so boring that I almost felt asleep.

   ChatGPT responds:

   The two sentences contain several grammatical errors:

   Subject Pronouns: 'Her and me' should be corrected to 'She and I', as these are the correct subject pronouns.

Double Negative: The phrase "didn't buy nothing" is a double negative. It should be "didn't buy anything".

Verb Tense: The phrase 'felt asleep' should be corrected to 'fell asleep' for proper verb usage.

A corrected version of the two sentences would be:

"She and I went to the store, but we didn't buy anything. The movie was so boring that I almost fell asleep."

Try this out with a longer example or a whole book!. You'll be impressed.

The Second Jewel: A Longer Prompt

We want to edit the following paragraph:

Many students struggles with math because they don't understands the basic concepts. Teachers often emphasize on memorization rather than understanding, which make learning difficult. If more attention were paid to the foundations, students would performs better in exams. This approach could helps them in long term.

We really should have many more sentences, but then reproducing the answer would be too long for his book——we will use longer examples in my other book: *The tediously long book of Writing Better.*

Magic prompt *Number the sentences. Edit sentence by sentence. Report by sentence, give reason for change:*

Many students struggles with math because they don't understands the basic concepts. Teachers often emphasize on memorization rather than understanding, which make learning difficult. If more attention were paid to the foundations, students would performs better in exams. This approach could helps them in long term.

Edited Paragraph with Reasons for Changes

1. **Original:** *Many students struggles with math because they don't understands the basic concepts.*
   Edited: *Many students struggle with math because they don't understand the basic concepts.*
   Reason: *Changed* struggles *to* struggle *to match the plural subject* students. *Changed* understands *to* understand *to match the subject* they.

2. **Original:** *Teachers often emphasize on memorization rather than understanding, which make learning difficult.*
   Edited: *Teachers often emphasize memorization rather than understanding, which makes learning difficult.*
   Reason: *Removed the unnecessary preposition* on *after* emphasize. *Changed* make *to* makes *to match the singular subject* which.

3. **Original:** *If more attention were paid to the foundations, students would performs better in exams.*
   Edited: *If more attention were paid to the foundations, students would perform better in exams.*
   Reason: *Changed* performs *to* perform *to match the modal verb* would.

4. **Original:** *This approach could helps them in long term.*
   Edited: *This approach could help them in the long term.*
   Reason: *Changed* helps *to* help *to match the modal verb* could. *Added* the *before* long term *for proper phrasing.*

And now the fun begins. Say, you agree with the edits of sentences 1 and 3, and want those changes done:
Do 1 and 3
You want all the changes done:
Do it all
Incredibly powerful!
How much you can learn from this! For every mistake, there is a correction, and an explanation why the correction was made. Pay attention to your tutor.

If the document is long, add *do not report on sentences with no edit* to the prompt.

B.5   Conclusion

With ChatGPT as your grammar tutor, you have a powerful tool at your disposal to improve your language skills. Whether you're just beginning your grammar journey or looking to refine your advanced understanding, ChatGPT is here to guide you every step of the way. Remember, practice makes perfect, and there's no question too small or too complex for ChatGPT to help you with!

C

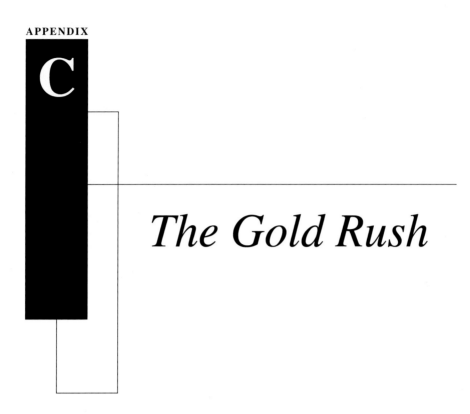

The Gold Rush

Answer the next forty exercises to become a winner of the

Gold Medal for Accomplishment

Figure C.1: Vecteezy Library

1. Correct the errors in the following sentence: "The car is parked on the side of the road in the building."
   Hint: *Refer to Section 1.4.*

2. Rewrite the sentence: "After we finished eating we went for a walk in the park and it was fun."
   Hint: *Check Section 2.5.*

3. Convert the following sentence from passive to active voice: "The project was completed by the team ahead of schedule."
   Hint: *See Section 3.3.*

4. Identify the ambiguity in this sentence and rewrite it to be clearer: "He saw the man with the telescope."
   Hint: *Refer to Section 4.1.*

5. Correct the sentence: "Walking down the street, the trees were beautiful."
   Hint: *See Section 8.2.*

6. Correct the errors in the following sentence: "The keys are under the mat in the kitchen."
   Hint: *Refer to Section 1.4.*

7. Rewrite the sentence: "She said she would arrive on time but she was late."
   Hint: *Check Section 2.5.*

8. Convert the following sentence from passive to active voice: "The results were analyzed by the researchers after the experiment."
   Hint: *See Section 3.3.*

9. Correct the sentence: "Running quickly, the finish line seemed far away."
   Hint: *See Section 8.2.*

10. Rewrite the sentence: "They left the meeting, and went to lunch, and discussed the project."
    Hint: *Check Section 2.5.*

Good start!

11. Convert the following sentence from passive to active voice: "The cake was baked by the chef in the afternoon."
    Hint: *See Section 3.3.*

12. Correct the sentence: "Jumping from the tree, the branch broke under her weight."
    Hint: *See Section 8.2.*

13. Correct the errors in the following sentence: "The cat sat beside the dog, and under the table."
    Hint: *Refer to Section 1.4.*

14. Rewrite the sentence: "He didn't finish his homework because he forgot, and the teacher was upset."
    Hint: *Check Section 2.5.*

15. Convert the following sentence from passive to active voice: "The presentation was given by the speaker at the conference."
    Hint: *See Section 3.3.*

16. Correct the sentence: "Reading the book, the time passed quickly."
    Hint: *See Section 8.2.*

17. Correct the errors in the following sentence: "The meeting was scheduled for at 10 a.m."
    Hint: *Refer to Section 1.4.*

18. Rewrite the sentence: "They packed their bags, and left the house, and drove to the airport."
    Hint: *Check Section 2.5.*

19. Convert the following sentence from passive to active voice: "The novel was read by millions of people."
    Hint: *See Section 3.3.*

20. Correct the sentence: "Driving down the highway, the scenery was breathtaking."
    Hint: *See Section 8.2.*

Up to bronze!

Figure C.2: Vecteezy Library

21. Correct the errors in the following sentence: "She looked the book under the table."
    Hint: *Refer to Section 1.4.*

22. Rewrite the sentence: "He finished his homework, and then went outside to play, and forgot about dinner."
    Hint: *Check Section 2.5.*

23. Convert the following sentence from passive to active voice: "The decision was made by the committee."
    Hint: *See Section 3.3.*

24. Correct the sentence: "Flying over the mountains, the view was stunning."
    Hint: *See Section 8.2.*

25. Correct the errors in the following sentence: "The car is parked in front of the house on the corner."
    Hint: *Refer to Section 1.4.*

26. Rewrite the sentence: "The project was challenging, and the team worked late, and they finally completed it."
    Hint: *Check Section 2.5.*

27. Convert the following sentence from passive to active voice: "The cake was eaten by the children."
    Hint: *See Section 3.3.*

28. Correct the sentence: "Standing in the rain, the umbrella kept her dry."
    Hint: *See Section 8.2.*

29. Correct the errors in the following sentence: "He was surprised in the results of the experiment."
    Hint: *Refer to Section 1.4.*

30. Rewrite the sentence: "She cooked dinner, and set the table, and called everyone to eat."
    Hint: *Check Section 2.5.*

    Up to silver!

Figure C.3: Vecteezy library

31. Convert the following sentence from passive to active voice: "The concert was attended by thousands of fans."
    Hint: *See Section 3.3.*

32. Correct the sentence: "Walking through the park, the flowers were in full bloom."
    Hint: *See Section 8.2.*

33. Correct the errors in the following sentence: "The document was signed at by all the parties."

Hint: Refer to Section 1.4.

34. Rewrite the sentence: "They cleaned the house, and then they took a break, and they watched a movie."
    Hint: Check Section 2.5.

35. Convert the following sentence from passive to active voice: "The award was received by the scientist for her groundbreaking research."
    Hint: See Section 3.3.

36. Correct the sentence: "While driving home, the radio played my favorite song."
    Hint: See Section 8.2.

37. Correct the errors in the following sentence: "He is interested for in learning new languages."
    Hint: Refer to Section 1.4.

38. Rewrite the sentence: "The sun set, and the stars appeared, and the night was calm."
    Hint: Check Section 2.5.

39. Correct the errors in the following sentence: "The conference was held on at the university."
    Hint: Refer to Section 1.4.

40. Rewrite the sentence: "He finished the book, and then he closed it, and he placed it on the shelf."
    Hint: Check Section 2.5.

Printed in the United States
by Baker & Taylor Publisher Services